# Adams County
# Mississippi

## Minutes *of the* Court Court

## 1802-1804

Prepared by:

The Mississippi Historical Records Survey
Service Division
Work projects Administration

Southern Historical Press, Inc.
Greenville, SC

This volume was reproduced from
An 1942 edition located in the
Publisher's private library,
Greenville, South Carolina

All rights reserved. No part of this publication
may be reproduced, stored in a retrieval system,
transmitted in any form, posted on to the web
in any form or by any means without the
prior written permission of the publisher.

Please direct all correspondence and orders to:

www.southernhistoricalpress.com
or
SOUTHERN HISTORICAL PRESS, Inc.
PO BOX 1267
375 West Broad Street
Greenville, SC   29601
southernhistoricalpress@gmail.com

Originally published: Jackson, MS. 1942
Reprinted by: Southern Historical Press, Inc.
Greenville, SC 2017
ISBN #0-89308-421-2
All rights Reserved.
*Printed in the United States of America*

PREFACE

The Historical Records Survey program was organized as a Nationwide project of the WPA to inventory State, county, and municipal archives, early American imprints, church records, and manuscripts in collections. In Mississippi the Historical Records Survey has operated as a unit of the State-wide Records Project in the Service Division, and has been sponsored by the Mississippi Department of Archives and History and some seventy county boards of supervisors. The Survey is being discontinued in order that its personnel may be divorted to activities which have a direct and unqualified relation to the war effort. However, this volume is being published since all data had been compiled for publication previous to the redirection of the activities of the project.

The preparation of inventories of county archives included the writing of administrative histories or essays which traced the development, analyzed the structure, and described the functions in each county of each of the agencies whose records were inventoried. It soon became obvious that if each inventory of county records was to depit the particular history, governmental organization, and records system of each county, it would be necessary to resort to the minutes of the county governing bodies for the source materials to do so. Experiments in transcribing pertinent passages from the minutes indicated that full coverage or uniform results could not be obtained by leaving the selection of the material to the judgment of field workers. For that reason, in 1939 and 1940, workers were assigned to transcribing in full, the minutes of the various governing bodies in some forty counties.

This volume, Transcription of the County Archives of Mississippi, No. 2, Adams County, Volume II, Minutes of the County Court, 1802-1804, is a transcription of the first volume of minutes of the county court kept in the basement storeroom of the Adams County courthouse. The volume, 16 inches high, nine inches wide, and one inch thick, is in poor condition. The cover and many of the pages are loose and torn and several of the pages are missing.

The minutes cover the period October 4, 1802 to September 9, 1804, and make accessible unpublished materials which furnish valuable and important information concerning the formative period in Mississippi history. Students, historians, genealogists, and others interested in basic documentary sources, will find a wealth of data embodied in this collection.

The county court was established February 26, 1802 by act of the first General Assembly of the Mississippi Territory. This act dissolved the court of general quarter sessions of the peace, the court of common pleas, and the court of probate established February 28, 1799 by Governor Winthrop Sargent and the Territorial Judges. (See Mississippi Historical Records Survey, Sargent's Code, A Collection of the

Original Laws of the Mississippi Territory Enacted 1799-1800 by Governor Winthrop Sargent and the Territorial Judges, Jackson, 1939, v, 168 pp. mimeo; and Mississippi Historical Records Survey, Transcription of the County Archives of Mississippi, No. 2, Adams County, Volume I, Minutes of the Court of General Quarter Sessions of the Peace, Jackson, 1942, xxii, 107 pp. mimeo.)

The court was given the judicial powers and duties in civil matters which had been vested in the court of common pleas and the administrative and police powers and duties which had been vested in both the court of common pleas and in the court of general quarter sessions of the peace.

In making the transcription of the original, the minutes were transcribed by project workers in longhand with pencil. The transcriptions were made word for word, line for line, and page for page in conformance with a manual of instructions. At the close of each day the material copied that day was proofread against the original and was transmitted to the State office where it was read and filed. If any portion of the transcription, such as handwriting or spelling, was thought to be deficient, the transcription was returned to the workers in the county for correction, verification, or clarification. The transcribors entered the word "/sic/" after each word misspelled in the original to indicate that the error was not made in the process of copying. After the transcribed copy was accepted as complete and correct, all editorial "/sic/'s" were deleted and the pencil transcription was then typed. The typed copy was proofread against the handwritten transcription, stencils were cut from the typed copy, and the stencils were then proofread against the typed copy.

Although the workers' copy was made line for line, the mimeographed version does not follow this rule. The transcription presented here is a word for word, paragraph for paragraph, page by page transcription. The page numbers of the original volume precede each page of transcription and the inclusive page numbers are carried in parentheses at the top of each mimeographed page. The pagination of the original was used to avoid the necessity of double page citations in the index to the original and published texts. The editorial device utilized to indicate the original page endings is a fine dotted line drawn entirely across the mimeographed page.

In the index an effort was made to include every place name and proper name and to group under subject heads, the significant items of information concerning the administrative and police powers and duties of the court.

General regulations and procedures applicable to all Historical Records Survey units in the 48 States have been followed in Mississippi. The officials of the WPA always gave the project their cordial support and assistance. The Survey gratefully acknowledges the interest and cooperation in this undertaking of the Adams County board of supervisors and of Dr. William D. McCain, Director of the Mississippi Department of Archives and History.

The original minutes were transcribed by Fannie Fleming and Lessie King, Historical Records Survey employees in Adams County. The transcriptions were edited by Andrew Brown, Assistant State Supervisor. The copy was typed and the stencils were cut by Lillie Ates, Mary Joe Tracy, and Marjorie Whitley. The index was prepared by Josephine Jones, Hazle Marshall, and Connie Pearson.

This, and the preceding volume, <u>Transcription of the County Archives of Mississippi, No. 2, Adams County, Volume I, Minutes of the Court of General Quarter Sessions of the Peace, 1799-1801</u>, have been published under the sponsorship of the Adams County board of supervisors.

The publications of the Survey are distributed without cost to State and local public officials and libraries in Mississippi, and to a limited number of libraries and governmental agencies outside the State. A list of these publications appears on page xx of this volume. Approximately 1,900 publications have been released by all units of the Survey throughout the Nation.

                                                  ROBERT E. STRONG
                                                  State Supervisor
                                                  Statewide Records Project

9 Bridges Building
Jackson, Mississippi
July 1942

At a County Court held for the County of Adams at the Courthouse thereof in the Town of Natchez, on Monday the fourth day of October in the year of our Lord, One thousand eight hundred & two.

Present
Samuel Brooks
James Ferrall
Joseph Irwin } Esquires
John Henderson

| | |
|---|---|
| William Dunbar Jr. Executor of the last will & Testament of James Orr, Dec$^d$ against | Plaintiff<br><br>In Case |
| Jeremiah Bass | Defendant |

Samuel Lusk as special Bail Surrendered the body of said Defendant into court in discharge of his recognizance and undertaking. The Defendant prayed into Custody

Lewis Kerr Esquire is admitted to practice as an attorney at Law in this Court having taken the usual Oaths, and having also produced a Licence from the Governor for the time being.

A mortgage from Thomas Tyler to Cavalier and Petit was proved to be the act and deed of the said Thomas Tyler by the Oath of Lyman Harding a subscribing witness thereto and Ordered to be Recorded.

Letters of Administration on the estate of Arthur Conner dec$^d$ is granted to William Scott, upon his entering into Bond with James Andrews his Security conditioned according to Law.

| | |
|---|---|
| James McMullen<br>Vs<br>Benjamin Carrol | Plaintiff<br>In /Blank/<br>Defendant |
| Same<br>Vs<br>Samuel Phipps | Plaintiff<br>In /Blank/<br>Defendant |

Ordered that the foregoing suit be dismissed the Plaintiff failing to appear to prosecute.

| | |
|---|---|
| Admors of Arabel Lewis<br>Against<br>Andrew White | Plaintiff<br>In /Blank/<br>Defendt. |

On the motion of the Plaintiff Ordered that the suit be dismissed at their costs.

An Indenture of Bargain and sale from Milling Wooley to George Cochran was proved to be the act and Deed of the said Milling Wooley by the Oath of Lyman Harding a subscribing witness thereto and Ordered to be Recorded.

(3-5)

| | |
|---|---|
| Abner S. Duncan | Plaintiff |
| Versus | In Case |
| Abram Martin | Defendant |

This day came the parties by their attorneys, and thereupon came also a Jury to wit, Robert Throgmorton Montford Calvit, Ezekiel Dewitt, Israel Luse, John King, Andrew Walker, George Killian, Abram Taylor, Moses Moore, Daniel Whittaker, Hamel McCollum, and Elisha Estridge who being elected tried and sworn well and truly to ~~enquire of de~~ try the issue Joined returned the following Verdict to wit, "We of the Jury find for the plaintiff" "Seventy five dollars in damage with cost of suit" Therefore, it is Considered by the Court that the plaintiff recover against the Said defend$^t$ his damages aforesaid in Manner and form by the Jurors in their Verdict aforesaid assessed and also his costs by him about his Suit in this behalf Expended and the defendant in Mercy &$^c$.

---

4

An Indenture of Bargain & Sale from Andrew Marshalk to George Cochran was proved to be the act and deed of the said Andrew by the Oath of Samuel S. Mahan a subscribing witness thereto and Ordered to be Recorded.

| | |
|---|---|
| Phoebe Martin | Plaintiff |
| Versus | In /Blank/ |
| John Wells | Defendant |

Ordered that this suit be continued until the next Term.

| | |
|---|---|
| William Gilberts, Exors. | Plaintiff |
| Versus | In /Blank/ |
| Job & Richard Cory | Defend$^t$ |

By consent Ordered that this suit be continued until the next Term.

| | |
|---|---|
| Mathow White, Exors. | Plaintiff |
| Versus | In /Blank/ |
| George Rapalje | Defendant |

This day came the Defendant by his attorney and the plaintiff being solemly called came not it is therefore Ordered that the Plaintiffs be non suited, and the Defend$^{ts}$ go hence without day and recove.. of the plaintiffs his costs by him about his defence in this behalf Suspended

---

5

| | |
|---|---|
| Henry Turner | Plaintiff |
| Versus | In /Blank/ |
| Elizabeth Shunk | Defendant |

Ordered that this Suit be dismissed It being so agreed by Plaintiff's attorney.

| | |
|---|---|
| John Wilson | Plaintiff |
| Against | In /Blank/ |
| Benjamin Monsantos, Exors. | Defendant |

Ordered that the pleadings in this cause be made up immediately which being done the same suit is Continued until next Term.

William Dunbar Jr. Exor. of          Plaintiff
   the last Will & Testament
   of James Orr dec^d              In Case
      Against
   Jeremiah Bass                   Defendant

Joseph Harris Comes into Court and undertakes for the Defendant that in, case he shall be cast in the suit he shall satisfy and pay the costs & condemnation of the court or render his body to prison in execution for the same or in case of failure there of that he the said Joseph will do it for him.

---

6

Richard Kirkland                   Plaintiff
   Against                         In /Blank/
Patrick Connely                    Defendant

On the motion of the Plaintiff by his attorney It is Ordered that this suit be dismissed.

John Holland                       Plaintiff
   Against                         In /Blank/
Samuel Reynolds                    Defendant
The Same                           Plaintiff
   against                         In /Blank/
Elias Fisher                       Defendant

By consent Ordered that the above suits be continued until the next Term.

William Mitchell                   Plaintiff
   against                         In /Blank/
Benjamine M. Stokes                Defendant

This day came the Defendant by his attorney an the plaintiff having been solemly called came not Therefore It is considered by the Court that the Plaintiff be non suited, and that the Defendant go hence without day and recover against the Plaintiff his costs by him about his defence in the behalf Expended.

        Court adj^d until to morrow morning 9
           of the clock.

---

7

      Tuesday October the 5th 1802 Court met
      according to adjournment.
        Present
         Samuel Brooks
         Caleb King       Esquires
         Joseph Irwin
         Jacob Guice

Ordered that John Bradley, James Cole, Gederon Hopkins, John Armstreet, John Verdiman, Israel Luse & Nathan Sayze Gent do view & mark out the nearest and best way for a road from Mr. Richard Swayze's Mill to Mr. James Ferrill's store near Capt Luse's from thence Continue the same road to Benjamine Farrow's Mill.

Also view and mark out the nearest & best way for a Road from Mr. John Lusk's ferry on the Homochitto to James Ferrill's Store near Capt. Luse's; from thence to the meeting-house near the North corner of Nathan Swayze's, improvement; and from thence to the Northwest corner of Jesse Hopper's improvement, and from thence to the main road leading from Willis's Creek to Natchez and make report thereof to the next Court according to Law.

Ordered that Jesse Harper, Batley E. Chaney, David Greenleaf, John Martin, Jonathan Rucker, Nathaniel Kinnison and Alexander Farrow Gent do view and mark out the nearest and best way for a road from Ellicotville to Jacob Guice,

Esq

---

Esquire and continue the same Road to Thomas Ward's; Also view and mark out such other roads necessary in Capt. Guice's district, and make report therefore to the next Court according to Law.

A report of a road from Natchez crossing St Catherines Creek at Glascock's bridge to E. Bonnell's ford of the Homochitto was returned in these words to wit "In compliance with an order of the Honourable Court for May Term 1802 we the undersigned have proceeded lay off and mark a road from Natchez crossing St Catherines' Creek at Glascock's to E. Bonnell's ford of the Homochitto In Testimony Whereof we have hereunto subscribed our names this tenth day of September A.D. One thousand Eight hundred and two Whereupon it is ordered that the said report be confirmed and that the said road be established.

Ordered that Jeremiah Coleman be appointed overseer of the road in the place of Prosper King.

Letters of admininistration on the estate of Williams decd is granted to Jesse Carter he having taken the Oath prescribed by Law and entered into and acknowledged Bond with Jeremiah Routh his security conditioned for his due and faithful administration of the said estate according to law.

---

| | |
|---|---|
| Hoggett & McClure | Plaintiff |
| Versus | Attachment |
| William Nolin | Defendant |

This day came the plaintiff and the ~~defendant~~ Sheriff having made return of the said attachment in the words to wit, "August 23$^d$ 1802 By virture of the within writ I proceeded to the former residence of the within named and under the direction of the Plaintiffs and at their risque attached one Yoke of Oxen" and the Defendant failing to appear and replevy the same Therefore It is considered by the court that the plaintiffs recover against the Said defendant sixty nine dollars ninety eight and half cents and also their costs by them about their suit in this behalf expended, and the defendant in Mercy & and it is ordered that the sheriff do make sale of the attached effects aforesaid and out of the money ensuing from such sale apply to the discharge of this Judg<sup>t</sup> and the overplus (if any) to the defendant.

An instrument of writing purporting to be a mortgage from Frederick Zerban to Samuel Watson was proved to be the act and deed of the said Frederick by the Oath of Abner L. Duncan a subscribeing witness thereto and Ordered to be Recorded

An Indenture of Bargain & Sale from David Ferguson & wife to William Wells was proved to be the act and deed of the Said David & wife by the oath of

---

10

Morris Custard a subscribing witness thereto & ordered to be Recorded.

| | |
|---|---|
| Barth<sup>m</sup> James, Admor. of the Estate of John Mc-Gurley | Plaintiff |
| against | In Case |
| John Wells | Defendant |

This day came the parties by their attorneys and thereupon came also a Jury to wit Robert Throgmorton, Montford Calvit, Ezekiel Dewit, Israel Luce, John King, Andrew Walker, George Killian, Abram Taylor, Moses Moore, Daniel Whitaker, Hansel McCollum, Elisha Estridge, who being elected tried and sworn well and truly to ty the issue joined upon their oath do say that the defendant did assume in manner & form as the plaintiff against him has declared and they do assess the plaintiff damages by reason thereof to fifty dollars and eighty one cents & costs of suit; Therefore It is consiedered by the Court that the Plaintiff recover against the said defendant his damages aforesaid in the manner & form by the Jurors in their verdict aforesaid assessed and also his costs by him about his suit in this behalf expended, and the defendant in Mercy &

| | |
|---|---|
| John Crow | Plaintiff |
| against | In debt |
| John E. Long | Defend<sup>t</sup> |

---

11

The defendant by James Wallace Esquire his attorney comes and prays oyer of the writing obligatory in the declaration mentioned which is read to him in these words to wit "Know all men by these presents that I John E. Long of Louisville and state of Kentucky am held and firmly bound unto John Crow or his heirs or assigne of s<sup>d</sup> state and county of Green in the penal sum of two hundred dollars to be paid on or before the 14<sup>th</sup> day of January 1800. Given under my hand & seal this twenty third of February One thousand seven hundred & ninety nine. The above condition of said obligation is such that if the above menshed, E. Long or his heirs or assigns pays or cause to be paid unto John Crow or his Heirs or assigns the just sum of Eighty three Dollars and twenty three cents and one third then the above obligation to be void otherwise to remain in full force and virtue Given under my hand seal the date above mentioned".

    his        John E. Long (seal)
Teste Bennan B Wilkins Isaac Hogland
    mark

Thoman Martin                    Plaintiff
    against                      In /Blank/
Tomasinan Sigvalt                Defendant

This day came the parties by their attorneys and thereupon came also a Jury to wit, Robert Throgmorton, Montford Calvit, Reubin Gibson, Israel Luse, John King, Andrew Walker, George Killian, Abram Taylor, Moses Moore, Daniel Whitaker, Hornself, McCollum & Elisha Estridge

who

12

who being elected tried and, sworn the truth to speak upon the issue joined returned the following verdict to wit, "We of the Jury find for the Plaintiff One hundred dollars in damages and costs of suit." Therefore, It is considered by that Court that the plaintiff recover against the said defendant his damage aforesaid in manner and form by the Jurors in their verdict aforesaid assessed and also his costs by him about his suit in this behalf expended & the said Defendant in Mercy &c

Samuel Owens (a Mullatto Freemans) deceased dying leaving a small estate, The Court doth order that Philander Smith take the said estate into his hands and the same Safely keep until the further order of the Court.

James Stewart is by the Court appointed Guardian to Alexander Calvet, Infant Orphan of Frederich Calvet decd whereupon he togeather with Robert Throgmorton and William A. Vandorn his securities entered into and acknowledged Bond Condition according to Law

Ordered, that Hampton White, Jesse Carter, Israel Smith, David Mitchell, Abner Green, William Conner, & Peter Presley sen. do view and mark out the most convenient way for roads in what is called Carter's District and make report thereof to Court

13

Bennet Truly                     Plaintiff
    Versus                       In Debt
Luke Whiting                     Defendant

This day came the parties by their attornies and the defendant acknowledged the plaintiff's action. Therefore it is considered by the Court that the plaintiff recover against the Said Defendant the sum of Eighty one dollars and also his costs by him about his suit in the behalf expended and the Defen$^d$ in Mercy &c The plaintiff agrees to stay over 4 months.

Ferguson & Wooley                Plaintiff
    against                      In /Blank/
James Findlay                    Defendant

Robert Throgmorton of this County comes into Court and undertakes for the Defendant that in case he shall be cast in this suit he shall satisfy and pay the costs and condemnation of the Court or render his body to prison in execution for the same or on failure thereof that he the said Robert will do it for him.

James Burney, Stephen Douglass, Patrick Connely, having been summoned as Jurors for this Term and failing to attend at the Solemly called It is ordered that the

---

14

be fined in the sum of ten dollars each and that Capear's pro fines do issue thereof.

Ordered that the Court do adjourn until tomorrow morning nine of the clock.

---

15

Wednesday the 6th October 1802
The Court met pursuant to adjt.
Present
Samuel Brooks
Caleb King
John Henderson Gent
Jacob Guice

An Indenture of Bargain & Sale from John Bullen, to Joseph Perkins was proved to be the act and deed of the said John by the Oath John Henderson one of the subscribing witnesses thereto and Ordered to be Recorded.

A Bond from the same to the same was proved by the same witness and ordered to be Recorded.

| Sutton Banks | Plaintiff |
| against | In /Blank/ |
| Samuel Morris | Defendt. |

Ordered that the suit be dismissed at the Defendant's costs.

An Indenture of bargain & sale from Francis Jones to William Dunbar was proved to be the act and deed of the /1 word illegible, crossed out/ said Francis by the oath of Lyman Harding and ordered to be Recorded.

---

16

| Ebenezer Rees | Plaintiff |
| against | In Case |
| Thomas Wilkins | Defendant |

This day came the parties aforesaid by their attornies and thereupon came also a Jury to wit Robert Throgmorton, Montford Calvit, Ezekiel Dewitt, Israel Luse, John King, Andrew Walker, George Killian, Abram Taylor, Moses Moore, Daniel Whitaker, Hansel McCollum, and Elisha Estridge

(16-18)

who being elected tried and sworn the truth to speak upon the issue joined upon their oath do say that the defendant did assume upon himself in manner and form as the plaintiff against him hath declared and they do assess the plaintiff's damages by reason of the assumption to forty dollars and ninety four cents besides costs. Therefore it is considered by the Court that the Plaintiff recover against the said defendant his dam$^s$ aforesaid in manner and form by the Jurors in the verdict aforesaid assessed and also his costs by him about his suit in this behalf expended and the defendant in Mercy &$^c$

17

Ezekiel DeWitt, having been summoned as a juror to the court, and failing to attend It is ordered that he be fined in the Sum of ten dollars unless he appear here during this term and make his excuses.

On the Motion of David Ker esquire clerk of the Court Ordered that William B. Elam be qualified as his Deputy.

| Ann Martin | Plaintiff |
| against | In Case |
| James Lomak | Defendant |

On the Motion of the Plaintiff by her counsel It is ordered that the suit be dismissed.

| James Moore | Plaintiff |
| against | In Case |
| The Same | Defendant |

On the motion of the Plaintiff by his Counsel It is ordered that this suit be Dismissed.

18

The complaint of James Blumer an apprentice against Winthrop Sargent Esq. his master for ill treatment laid over & continued until Friday next.

| Robert Abrams, Adm$^{or}$. &$^c$ | Plaintiff |
| against | In case |
| John Ferguson | Defendant |

This day came the parties by their attornies and thereupon came also a Jury to wit Robert Throgmorton, Montford Calvit, Ezekiel DeWitt, Israel Luce, John King, Andrew Walker, George Killian, Abram Taylor, Moses Moore, Daniel Whitaker, Hansol McCollum, and Elisha Estridge who being elected tried and sworn , well and truly to try the issue joined upon their oath do say that the defendant did assume upon himself in manner and form as the plaintiff against him hath declared and they do assess the plaintiffs damages by reason of that assumption to twenty dollars and seventy five cents besides costs, Therefore It is considered by the court that the plaintiff recover against the Said defendant his damages aforesaid in manner and form by the Jurors their verdict aforesaid assessed and also

---

his costs by him about his Suit in this behalf expended and the defendant in mercy &c

| | |
|---|---|
| Ezekiel Dewitt | Plaintiff |
| against | In Debt |
| Thomas Nichols | Defendant |
| The Same | Plaintiff |
| against | In Debt |
| Martin Owens | Defendant |
| Samuel Headey | Plaintiff |
| against | In Debt |
| James McMullen | Defendant |

Judgment by Default.

An Indenture of Bargain and sale from Ebenezer Rees to John Henderson was acknowledged by the said Ebenezer to be his act and deed and ordered to be Recorded

| | |
|---|---|
| Nathaniel Ivy | Plaintiff |
| against | In Debt |
| Ebenezer Reese | Defendant |

This day came the parties by their attornies and the defendant acknowledged the plaintiff's action, Therefore it is considered by the Court that the plaintiff recover

against

---

against the Said defendant One hundred & seven dollars & 98½ cts. and also his costs by him about his suit in the behalf expended and in mercy &c

William Barland against Ebenezer Rees continued until Saturday next.

| | |
|---|---|
| John P. Perkins | Plaintiff |
| against | In /Blank/ |
| Ebenezer Rees | Defendant |

This day came the parties by their attornies and the defendant acknowledged the plaintiff's action. Therefore it is considered by the Court that the plaintiff recover against the said defendant sixty three dollars and seventy nine cents and also his cost by him about his suit in the behalf expended and the defendant in Mercy &c.

| | |
|---|---|
| William Boll | Plaintiff |
| against | In Debt |
| Lewis Evans | Defend$^t$ |

This day came the parties by their attornies and the defendant acknowledged the plaintiff's action. Therefore it is considered by the court that the Plaintiff recover against the said defendant the sum of Ninety six dollars and four and four and one half cents and also his costs by him about his suit in this behalf expended and the defendant in Mercy &c. Note: This Judgment is for the benifit of James Melson.

James McCibbin      Plaintiff
   against             In /Blank/
Ebenezer Rees      Defendant

On the motion of the Plaintiff by his counsel ordered that this suit be dismissed.

Ann Martin against James Lennox. It appearing to the Court that the defendant was subponad as a witness in the suit of said Martin against Ezekiel Dewitt. And it also appearing that he was served with a process at the suit of the said Ann. It is Ordered that he be discharged therefrom. The same being executed while on his attendance.

Ordered that the Court be adj$^d$ until tomorrow morning 9 of the clock.

---

Thursday Oct$^o$ 7th 1802
The Court met according to adjournment
    Present
      Samuel Brooks
      Ford$^d$ L. Claiborne    Esquires
      William Darby
      Jacob Guice

James Carrick      Plaintiff
   against            In Debt
Patrick Foley      Defend$^t$

This day came the parties aforesaid by their attornies and thereupon came also a Jury to wit Robert Throgmorton, Ezekiel Dewitt, Israel Luce, John King, Andrew Walker, George Killian, Moses Moore, Daniel Whitaker Jeremiah Routh, Hansel McCollum, Elisha Estridge, and Reuben, Gibson, who being elected tried and sworn well & truly to try the issue joined returned the following verdict to wit "We of the jury find that the said Patrick hath not paid to the said James Carrick the said sum of three hundred and forty dollars with all legal interest thereon due in such manner and form as the s$^d$ Patrick in pleading hath alledged and therefore find for the Plt. the said debt of three hundred and forty dollars

                                                             in

---

in the declaration mentioned and one hundred and forty seven dollars and twenty nine cents damages for the detention of the same with costs of suit" Therefore it is considered by the court that the Plaintiff recover against the defendant his debt and damages afores$^d$ in manner and form by the jurors in their verdict aforesaid assessed and also his costs by him about his Suit in this behalf expended and the defendant in Mercy &c.

Ordered that Thomas Wilkins, William Foster, John Grafton, Robert Dunbar, Emanuel Madden, William Lemon and John Wilie, Gent. do view and mark out the necessary roads in the district of Capt. William Darby Company and make report thereof to the next court according to Law.

In pursuance of the act of Assembly for that purpose, the Court proceeded to nominate the number of Jurors for the county as directed by the said act, to attend at the next superior court for the district of Adams, whereupon the following housekeepers free holders were nominated to wit Col$^o$ John Steele, Sutton Banks, William G. Forman, Peter Walker, James McIntosh,

Thomas Reid, David Holt, Joseph Newman, Samuel Neil, John Garrach, Lewis West, Robert Dunbar, James Bass, Ebenezer Rees, David Gibson, Capt. John Wade, Andrew Marschalk, John Bowles, Joseph Calvit, Christopher Miller, Nathaniel Tomlinson, Andrew Bell, Simpson Holmes, James Foster, William Foster, Anthony Hoggart, Wilford Hoggart and Job Routh and it is ordered that a writ of venire facias do issue to the Sheriff accordingly.

Ordered that Archibald Lewis, Reubin Gibson, Joseph Calvit, Ezekiel Dewitt, Thomas Reid and Daniel Whitaker, Gent do view and mark out the different roads necessary in the district of Capt. Duncan's Company and make report thereof to the next court according to Law.

| | |
|---|---|
| Elijah Craig | Plaintiff |
| against | In Case |
| Miguel Sollivellas | Defendant |

This day came the parties by their attornies and thereupon came also a Jury to wit, Robert Throgmorton, Ezekiel Dewitt, Israel

Luse, John King, Andrew Walker, George Killian, Moses Moore, Daniel Whitaker, Jeremiah Routh, Hansel McCollum, Elisha Estridge, Reubin Gibson who being elected tried and sworn the truth to speak upon the issue joined returned the following verdict to wit "We the Jury find that the defend$^t$ did assume in the manner and form as the Plt. in his declaration hath alledged and find for the plaintiff two hundred in damages and costs of suit." Therefore it is considered by the court that the plaintiff recover against the said defendant his damages aforesaid in manner and form by the Jurors in their verdict aforesaid assessed also his costs by him about his suit in this behalf expended and the said defendant in Mercy &$^c$.

| | |
|---|---|
| Nathaniel Tomlinson | Plaintiff |
| against | Upon as att$^a$ |
| Robert Knox | Defendant |

On the motion of the defendant by his counsel to quash the attachment awarded Therein The parties being fully heard, It is the opinion of the Court that the Said attachment and the proceedings thereon are defective and illegal upon the face of it, and that the Same be quashed From which opinion and Judgment of the Court the Plaintiff prayed an appeal to the next Superior court of Law to be holden for the District of Adams, which is granted upon his giving Bonds with security in the penalty of one hundred dollars conditioned according to Law.

Ordered that the Court do adjorun until tomorrow morning 9 of the clock.

---

Friday the 8th day of Oct. 1802
The Court met pursuant to adjournm$^t$
Present
Samuel Brooks
Jacob Guice       Esquires
James Neilson
John Henderson

An Inventory and appraisement of the estate of William N. Galbraith deceased was returned and ordered to be Recorded.

William B. Smith                Plaintiff
   against                    In [Blank]
John & William Wells            Defendant

This day came the parties by their attornies and thereupon came also a Jury to wit, Robert Throgmorton, Ezekel Dewitt, Israel Luce, John King, Andrew Walker, Steven Stevenson, Moses Moore, Daniel Whitaker, Jeremiah Routh, Hansel McCollum, Elisha Estridge, Reuben, Gibson & Abram Taylor, who being elected tried and sworn the truth to speak upon the issue joined returned the following verdict to wit "We the Jury find for the plaintiff thirty six dollars and fifty cents with costs of Suit." Therefore it is considered by the court that the plaintiff recover against the Said

---

defendants his damages aforesaid in manner and form by the jurors in their verdict aforesaid assessed, and also his costs by him about his suit in this behalf expended and the said defendants in Mercy &c.

Rebecca McCabe                  Plaintiff
   Versus                     In [Blank]
Thomas Hutchins                 Defendant

Aguments of demurrer to plaintiffs replication to the defendants plea in abatement ordered to be brought on at three o'clock this evening.

Ordered that John Ford, Nathaniel Kinnison, Barley Chaney, William Kimson, Christopher Guice, Abram Guice, and Jesse Harper Gent do view and mark out the necessary roads in the district of Capt Guice's Company and make report thereof to the next court court agreeably to Law.

Robert Moore & Co.              Pltf
   Versus                     In [Blank]
William B. Smith                Deft.

Dismissed each party paying half the costs by consent.

Alexander Moore, Exors.        Plaintiffs
    against
Hardress Ellis                 Defendant

Refered to Sutton Banks and James Barr, Gent and agree that their award be made the Judgment of the Court, and that the same be returned to the clerks office within one month and execution to issue thereon which is ordered accordingly.

Hardress Ellis                 Plaintiff
    against
Benjamine Carrol               Defendant

Continued by consent - and it is agreed that the Plaintiff shall not bring this suit to trial in the absence of two witnesses of the defendants.

James Williamson               Plaintiff
    against
Maurice Stackpool, Exors.      Defendant

Dismissed each party to pay their own costs.

Benjamine Kitchen              Plaintiff
    Versus
Bryan Bruin                    Defendant

Refered to William T. McCormick and Samuel Postlethwait Gent and agree that their award be made the Judgment of

the

the Court, and to be returned in the Clerk's office, and execution to issue thereon, which is ordered accordingly.

Phobe Calvit                   Plaintiff
    Vs
John Brow                      Defend$^t$

By consent ordered that this suit be continued until next Term.

Timberlake & Hancock           Plt.
    against                Att$^a$
James Green                    Defend$^t$

On the motion of the plaintiff ordered that this suit be dismissed.

Christ$^o$ Lee                 Plt.
    against                In [Blank]
John Cammack                   Deft.

This day came the plaintiff by his attorney and thereupon came also a Jury to wit, Robert Throgmorton, Ezekiel Dewitt, Israel Luce, John King, Andrew Walker, Steven Stevenson, Moses Moore, Daniel Whitaker, Jeremiah Routh, John Eldergill, Elisha Estridge, Ruobin Gibson, Abram Taylor, who being elected tried and sworn well and truly to enquire of

damages

damages in this suit returned "We of the Jury find for the Plt. fifty nine dollars and four cents in damages, and costs of suit." Therefore it is considered by the Court that the plaintiff recover against the Said defendant his damages aforesaid in manner and form by the Jurors in their verdict aforesaid assessed, and also the costs by him about his suit in this behalf expended and the defendant in Mercy &$^c$.

 I do hereby transfer the within Judgment to Samuel S. Mahon, he having satisfied me for the same, witness my hand and seal this 1$^{st}$ Nov. 1802
         Signed
         Christopher Lee, L.S.

 Ebenezer Rees      Plaintiff
  against
 Anthony Benedict     Defendant

This day comes the plaintiff by his attorney and thereupon came also a Jury to wit Robert Throgmorton, Ezekiel Dewitt, Israel Luce, John King, Andrew Walker, Steven Stevenson, Moses Moore, Daniel Whitaker, Jeremiah Ruth, John Eldergill, Elisha Estridge, Ruebin Gibson and Abram Taylor who being duly elected tried and sworn well

                 and

and truly to enquire to enquire of damages in this suit upon their oath do say that the plaintiff hath sustained damages by reason of the defendants' non performance of his promise and undertaking in the declaration mentioned to the amount of twenty five dollars eighty seven and one half cents, and one half cents besides costs. Therefore it is considered by the court that the plaintiff recover against the Said defendant his damages aforesaid by the Jurors in their verdict aforesaid, assessed and also his costs by him about his suit in this behalf expended and the defendant in Mercy &$^c$.

 John Potter       Plaintiff
  against
 Peter Bryan Bruin     Defendant

This day came the Plaintiff by his attorney and thereupon came also a Jury to wit: Robert Throgmorton, Ezekiel Dewitt, Israel Luce, John King, Andrew Walker, Steven Stevenson, Moses Moore, Daniel Whitaker, Jeremiah Ruth Hansol McCollum, Elisha Estridge, Reubin Gibson, Abram Taylor, who being elected tried and sworn well and to enquire of damages in this suit upon their oath do say that the plaintiff hath sustained damages by reason of the defendants nonperformance of his assumption in the declaration mentioned to the amount of fifty three dollars & five cents besides costs, Therefore it is considered by the Court that the plaintiff recover against the said defendant his damages aforesaid in manner and form by the Jurors in their verdict aforesaid assessed and also his costs by him about his writ in this behalf expended and the defendant Mercy &c.

John Ferguson          Plaintiff
   against
John Stillee            Defendant

This day came the plaintiff by his attorney and thereupon came also a Jury to wit, Robert Throgmorton, Ezekiel Stevenson, Moses Moore, Daniel Whitaker, Jeremiah Routh, Hansel McCollum, Elisha Estridge, Roubin Gibson, Abram Taylor, who being elected tried and sworn well and truly to enquire of damages in this suit upon their oath do say that the plt. hath sustained damage by reason of the Defts non performance, of the promise and undertaking in the declaration to the amount of forty four dollars six & one half cents besides his cost of suit Therefore it is considered by the court that the plaintiff recover against the Said defendant

his damage aforesaid by the jurors in their verdict aforesaid assessed and also his costs by him about his suit in this behalf expended and the said defendant in Mercy &c.

Ordered that the caveat against an instrument of writing purporting to be the will of Elias Bonnell deceased together with the motion for letters of administration to Lewis Shelton &c be entered on the minutes; which are in the words to wit- "The worshipful the Justices of the County Court of Adams now sitting will not let the instrument of writing lately produced to your worships purporting to be the last will and testament of Elias Bonnell dec[d] receive probate in your court nor grant letters testamentary to any person or persons, who may be named Executors in Said instrument of writing. 1st Because the dec[d] was not of sound mind at the time of executing said instrument; 2nd Because of the evedent injustice said instrument is calculated to work; 3rd Because said instrument is defective in point of form; 4th Because it does not pursue the ordinance of this Territory in as much as there are not

three subscribing witnesses who attest Said Instrument.

Samuel S. Mahon attorney for Lewis Shelton Motion also for administration to be granted to Lewis Shelton (who is intermarried with Mary Boneldaughter of Elias Bonel dec[d] for the Safe keeping of the effects of the dec[d] Samuel S. Mahon Attorney for Lewis Shelton, Whereupon It is ordered that the Same be argued on Monday morning next.

Thomas Martin                    Plaintiff
    against
Thomasina Sigvalt                Defendant

The defendant by her attorney prayed an appeal to the next Superior Court of Law to be holden for Adams District which is granted upon her giving Bond and Security in the penalty of two hundred dolls, conditioned according to Law.

Ordered that Col° John Steele, George Fitzgerald, Major Richard King, Peter Walker, esquire, Lewis Evans esquire, Mr. Job Routh, & Mr. George Overaker do view and mark out necessary roads to be opened, repaired or altered in Capt Ferdinand L. Claiborn's District and make report thereof to the next Court according to Law.

---

An Indenture of Bargain and sale from Robert Carter to Joseph Perkins was proved to be the act and deed of the Said Robert by the oath of Patrick Foley a witness thereto subscribed, & Ordered to be Recorded.

Stephen Stephenson               Plaintiff
    against
Juan Rodrigroes                  Defendant

This day came the Plaintiff by his attorney & thereupon came also a Jury to wit Robert Throgmorton, Ezekiel Dewitt, Israel Luse, John King, Andrew Walker, Moses Moore, /one word illegible, crossed out/ Daniel Whitaker Jeremiah Routh, Hansel McCollum, Elisha Estridge, Rubin Gibson & Abram Taylor who being elected tried and sworn well and truly to enquire of damages in this suit upon their oath, do say that the plaintiff hath sustained damages by reason of the defendant's nonperformance of his promise and undertaking in the declaration mentioned to the amount of one Hundred and fourteen dollars sixty cents besides his costs of suit.
Therefore it is considered by the Court that the plaintiff recover against the said defendant his damages aforesaid in manner and form by the

---

Jurors in their verdict aforesaid and also his costs by him about his suit in this behalf expended and the defendant in Mercy &c.

John Wells                       Plaintiff
    Versus                       Atty
John Holland                     Defendant

This day came the plaintiff by his attorney and thereupon came also a Jury to wit Robert Throgmorton, Ezek¹ Dewitt, Israel Luse, John King, Andrew Walker, Moses Moore, Daniel Whitaker, Jeremiah Routh, Hansel McCollum, Elisha Estridge, Reubin Gibson, /one word illegible, crossed out/ and Abram Taylor, who being elected tried and sworn well and truly to enquire of damages in this suit upon their oath do say that the plaintiff hath sustained damages by reason of the defendants' nonperformance of his promise and undertaking in the declaration ment^d to the amount of two hundred and twenty seven dollars and nine cents besides Cost, Therefore it is considered by the Court that the plaintiff recover against the said defendant his damages aforesaid in manner & form by the Jurors in their verdict aforesaid assessed and also his costs by him about his Suit in this behalf expended, and the Said defendant in Mercy &c. And it is further considered and ordered that the money and property in the possession of Samuel Brooks belonging to the defendant which the said

Samuel

---

## 38

Samuel as Garnishee hath confessed to have had in his hands and posession at the time of the execution of the said attachment be delivered to the sheriff of Adams County and that the lott and premises belonging to the Said John Holland returned by the Sheriff on the said attachment to be attached be condemned to satisfy the residue of that Said debt and costs, and the Sheriff of this County is hereby ordered to sell and dispose of the said property and lott and premises at publick sale he first advertising the time of the sale in one of the public papers printed in this Territory &c.

An Indenture of Bargain and sale from Robert Moore to Samuel S. Mahon was proved to be the act and deed of the Said Robert by the oath of David Mickie one of the subscribing witnesses thereto and ordered to be Recorded.

An Indenture of Bargain and Sale from George Cochran, to Samuel S. Mahon is as proved to be the act and deed of the Said George Cochran by the oath of James Wilkins a subscribing witness thereto and ordered to be Recorded.

---

## 39

An Indenture of Bargain and Sale from Patrick Connely to James Wallace was proved to be the act and deed of the Said Patrick Connely by the by the oath of John Eldergill one of the subscribing witnesses thereto and ordered to be Recorded.

    Rebecca McCabe             Plaintiff
        against
    Thomas Hutchins         Defendant

This day came the parties by their Attornies and the Demurrer to the plaintiff Replecation to the Deft^s plea in abatement being argued, It is the opinion of the Court that the Law is for the Defendant, Therefore it is considered by the Court that the Plt^s suit be dismissed and that the defendant recover against her his costs by him about his ~~suit~~ defence in this behalf expended and go hence without day.

Ordered that the court be adjourned until tomorrow morning nine of the clock

Saturday October the 9th 1802
The Court met according to adjournment
                Present
                Samuel Brooks
                Ferdinand L. Claiborn Esqrs
                Abner Green

An Indenture of Bargain and sale from Robert Moore to Philip Gearaighty and Richard Orrilly was proved to be the act and deed of the said Robert by the oath of Abner L. Duncan Esquire and ordered to be Recorded.

An Instrument of writing purporting to be a Mortgage from George Lawing to Ferdinand L. Claiborne was proved to be the act and deed of the said George by the oath John Nichols and ordered to be Recorded.

An Indenture of Bargain and Sale from John Foster, to George Lawing was proved to be the act and deed of the Said John ~~Nichols~~ Foster by the oath of John Nichols and Ordered to be Recorded.

An Indenture of Bargain and Sale from George King to Anthony Hutchins was proved

to be the act and deed of the Said George by the oath of Samuel McDowell a witness thereto and ordered to be Recorded.

A Power of Attorney from Francis Jones to William T. McCormick was proved to be the act and deed of the Said Francis by the oath of James Dunlap and ordered to be Recorded.

The last Will and Testament of William Vousdan decd was proved to be the act and deed of the said William by the oath of Ferdinand L. Claiborne one of the Subscribing witnesses thereto and ordered to be Recorded Whereupon David Ker and William T. McCormick two of the Exors therein named made oath for the due performance of the duty as Executors aforesaid according to Law.

| Henry Pearson | Plaintiff |
| against | In Case |
| Ebenezer Rees | Defendant |

This day came parties by their attornies and thereupon came also a Jury to wit Robert Throgmorton, Ezekiel Dewitt, John King, Andrew Walker, George Killian, Moses Moore, Daniel Whitaker, Jeremiah Routh, John Eldergill, Elisha Estridge, Reubin

Gibson and Abram Taylor who being elected tried and sworn well and truly to try the issue joined upon their oath do say that the Defendant did not assume upon himself in manner and form as the plaintiff hath declared, Therefore it is considered by the Court the [one word illegible, crossed out] Defendant go hence without day and recover against the Said Plt. his costs by him about his defence in this behalf expended and that the Plt. together with his false clamour be in Mercy &c

| | |
|---|---|
| William Barland | Plaintiff |
| against | In Case |
| Ebenezer Reese | Defendant |

This day came the parties by their attornies, and the Defendant acknowledged the Plaintiffs' action, Therefore it is considered by the Court that the plaintiff recover against the Said Defendant the Sum of three hundred and twenty eight dollars and twenty nine cents, the dam$^{gs}$ in the declaration mentioned and also his costs by him about his suit in this behalf expended and the said Defendant in Mercy &$^c$

---

43

Leonard Claiborne et al against John Overaker Continued by consent

Samuel Flower vs Polser Shilling Continued for Plt. to bring his Bill of discovery in Equity prior to the next term of this Court, if not to be non Suited &$^c$

| | |
|---|---|
| Rebecca McCabe | Plaintiff |
| Versus | In Trover & Conversion |
| Nathaniel Tomlinson | Defendant |

This day came the parties by their attorneys and there upon came also a Jury to wit Robert Throgmorton, Ezekiel Dewitt, John King, Andrew Walker, George Killian, Moses Moore, Daniel Whitaker, Jeremiah Routh, John Eldergill, Elisha Elderidge, Rubin Gibson, and Abram Taylor, who being Elected tried and sworn the truth to speak upon the issue joined returned the following verdict to wit, "We of the Jury find that the defendant is guilty in manner and form as the plaintiff has alledged against him and assess the plaintiff damages to one hundred and forty five dollars & fifty cents and cost of suit-." Therefore it is, considered by the Court that the plaintiff recover against the said Defendant her damages aforesaid

---

44

in Manner and form by the Jurors in their verdict aforesaid assessed and also his costs by him about his suit in this behalf Expended and the said Deft. in Mercy &$^c$ -

An Indenture of Bargain and Sale from John Foster to Ebenezer Rees was proved to be the act and deed of the Said John Foster by the oath of John Brabston one of the subscribing witnesses thereto and ordered to be Recorded.

An Indenture of Bargain and Sale from same to same proved by the same witness and Ordered to be Recorded.

Ordered that Stephen Douglass, Bennett Truly, Thomas Tyler, James Dinwiddy, Anthony Daugherty, Samuel Morris, Jeremiah Routh, do view and mark out the Different Roads necessary in Capt. Wade's District and make report thereof to the next Court according to law.

45

The Complaint of James Blumon an apprentice against Wynthrop Sargent Esquire his master for ill treatment &c laid over until Monday next.
Ordered that the Court be adj$^t$ until Monday Morning next.

46

Monday Morning Oct$^o$ 11th 1802
The Court Met according /one word illegible, crossed out/ to adjournment
Present
  Samuel Brooks
  John Henderson
  James Neilson
  Abner Green
  Joseph Sessions

William Mitchell      Plaintiff
  against
Thomas Hutchins      Defendant

This day came the parties by their attornies, and the Defendant acknowledged the plaintiff's action for one hundred and Eight dollars Therefore it is considered by the Court that the Plaintiff recover against the said defendant the said one hundred and eight dollars and also his Costs by him about his suit in this behalf expended and the said Defendant in Mercy &c.

47

James Ashworth      Plaintiff
  against             In /Blank/
Thomas Tyler      Defendant

This day came the parties by their attornies and the Defendant acknowledged the plaintiff's action, Therefore it is considered by the Court that the Plaintiff recover against the Said Defend$^t$ this sum of One hundred and twenty nine dollars and thirty nine Cents and also his Costs by him about his suit in this behalf expended and the Said Defendant in Mercy &c.

The Same      Plaintiff
  Vs
The Same      Defendant

This day came the parties by their attornies and the Defendant acknowledged the plaintiff's action Therefore it is Considered by the Court that the plaintiff recover against the said defendant the sum of three hundred and twenty Seven dollars and sixty five Cents and also his Costs by him about his Suit in this behalf expended and the Defendant in Mercy &c.

Samuel Flowers against Nathaniel Tomlinson Continued

Rebecca McCabe            Plaintiff
   against
Darius Moffett             Defendant

This day came the parties by their attornies and the Defendant acknowledged the plaintiff's action for one cent and the costs Therefore it is considered by the Court that the plaintiff recover against the Defendant the Said one cent and also /one word illegible, crossed out/ Costs by her about her Suit in this behalf expended and the Defendant in Mercy &c.

    Ordered that Abner Green, Ferdinand L. Claiborne, and Walter Burling & James Neilson, Esquires be requested to lay off the prison bounds in this County on Saturday next.

    An Indenture of Bargain and Sale from Joseph Ford Senior to John King was

proved to be the act and deed of the said Joseph by the oath of James Jones one of the Subscribing witnesses thereto and Ordered to be Recorded.

John Dewitt            Plaintiff
   against
Martin Owens           Defendant

Judgment confessed subject to any defalcation which may be made by the Clerk of this Court

Samuel Flower           Plaintiff
   against
Jesse Greenfield         Defendant

This day came the parties by their attornies and the defendant acknowledged the plaintiff's action for Forty four dollars and the Costs, Therefore it is considered by the Court that the plaintiff recover against the said defendant the Said sum of forty four dollars and also his costs by him about his suit in this behalf expended and the Said defendant in Mercy &c.

    Bill of sale from John Nicklass attorney in fact for Alexander Porter to William Kenner was proved to be the act & deed of the Said John by the Oath of James Hogg and ordered to be Recorded.

William Barrow          Plaintiff
   against
Whiting & Stokes        Defend$^t$

This day came the plaintiff by his attorney and thereupon came also a Jury to wit John Ferguson, John Shackler, Ezekiel Dewitt, Israel Luse, John King, Moses Moore, Daniel Whitaker, Roubin Gibson, Abram Taylor, George Killian, Robert Throgmorton, Montford Calvit who being elected, tried and sworn well and truly to Enquire of Damages in this suit returned "We the Jury find for the plaintiff ninety three dollars and twenty four Cents in damages & Cost of suit" Therefore it is considered by the

Court that the plaintiff recover against the said defendants his damages aforesaid in manner and form by the Jurors in their verdict aforesaid assessed and also his costs by him about his suits in this behalf expended and the said Defendants in Mercy &c.

| | |
|---|---|
| John Rasselly | Plaintiff |
| Vs | |
| Patrick Connely Et al | Defendants |

This day came the plaintiff by his attornies and thereupon came also a Jury to wit (same Jury as last) who being elected tried and sworn well and truly to enquire of Damages in this suit returned "We of the Jury find for the plaintiff one houndred and twenty two Dollars and thirty five Cents in damages & Costs of suit"- Therefore It is considered by the Court that the plaintiff recover against the Said defendants his Damages afore$^d$ in Manner and form by the Jurors in their verdict aforesaid assessed and also his costs by him about his suit in this behalf expended and the Defts in Mercy &c.

---

| | |
|---|---|
| Huhey Smith | Plaintiff |
| against | |
| Thomas Massey | Defendant |

This day came the plaintiff by his attorney and thereupon came also a Jury to wit (same Jury as last) who being elected tried and sworn well and truly to enquire of Damages in this suit returned the following verdict to wit "We of the Jury find for the plaintiff One hundred and Eight dollars - 92 cents in Damages and costs of suit" Therefore it is considered by the Court that the plaintiff recover against the said defendant his damages aforesaid in Manner and form by The Jurors in their verdict aforesaid assessed and also his Costs by him about his Suit in this behalf expended and the Said defendant in Mercy &c.

| | |
|---|---|
| Martain Huffman | Plaintiff |
| against | |
| James Elliott | Defendants |

This day came the plaintiff by

---

his Attorney and thereupon came also a Jury to wit (Same Jury as last) Who being elected tried and sworn well and truly to enquire of damages En this suit returned "We of the Jury find for the plaintiff one cent in damages & Costs of suit." Therefore is is considered by the Court that the plaintiff recover against the said defendant his damages aforesaid in Manner and form by the Jurors in their verdict aforesaid assessed and also his Costs by him about his Suit in this behalf expended and the Said defendant in Mercy &c.

| | |
|---|---|
| Windsor Pipes | Plaintiff |
| against | |
| John Bullon | Defendant |

This day came the plaintiff by his Attorney and thereupon came also a Jury to wit (Same Jury as last) who being elected tried & sworn well, and truly to enquire of damages in this suit Returned, "We of the Jury find for the plaintiff one cent in damages and costs of suit" Therefore it is considered by the Court that the plaintiff recover against the said defendant his

damages aforesaid in Manner and form by the Jurors in Their verdict aforesaid assessed and also his Costs by him about his suit in this behalf expended and that said defendant in Mercy &c.

James & John Perrelliatte     Plaintiff
    against
Francisco Millan     Defendant

This day the plaintiffs by their attorney and thereupon came also a Jury to wit (same Jury as last) who being elected tried and sworn well and truly to enquire of damages in this suit returned "We of the Jury find for the plaintiff three hundred and thirty eight dollars & fifty six and one half cents in damages and costs of Suit." Therefore it is considered by the Court that the plaintiffs recover against the said defendant their damages aforesaid in manner and form by the Jurors in their verdict aforesaid assessed and also their Costs by them about their suit in this behalf expended and the defendant in Mercy &c.

Thomas Irwin     Plaintiff
    against
Thomas Dorrock     Defendant

This day came the plaintiff by his attorney and thereupon came also a Jury to wit (same Jury as last) who being elected tried and Sworn well and truly to Inquire of damages in this suit returned "We of the Jury find for the plaintiff fifty eight dollars and thirty cents and damages by the Court that the Pltf recover against the said defendant his damages aforesaid by the Jurors in their verdict aforesaid assessed and also his costs by him about his Suit in this behalf expended and the said defendant in Mercy &c

Rood & Ford     Plaintiff
    against
Thomas Dorrock     Defendant

This day came the plaintiffs by their attorney and thereupon came also a Jury to wit (same Jury as last) who being elected tried and sworn

well and truly to enquire of damages in this suit returned "We of the Jury find for the plts. Eight one dollars and twenty cents in dams. and Costs of suit"- Therefore it is considered by the Court that the plaintiffs recover against the said defendant their damages aforesaid in Manner and form by the jurors in their verdict aforesaid assessed and also their costs by them about their suit in the behalf expended and the said defendant in Mercy &c.

  John Dewitt        Plt.
   against
  Thomas Nicholls      Deft.

This day came the plaintiff by his attorney & Thereupon came also a Jury to wit (same Jury as last) who being elected tried and sworn well and truly to enquire of damages in this suit returned "We of the Jury find for the plaintiff fifty two dollars and twenty one cents in Damages and costs of Suit". Therefore it is considered by the court that the plaintiff recover against the said defendant his damages aforesaid in Manner and form by the Jurors in

---

57

their verdict aforesaid assessed also his costs by him about his suit in this behalf expended and the said defendant in Mercy &c.

  Abija Hunt         Plaintiff
   against
  McWilliams & Kitchens    Defendants

This day came the plaintiff by his Attorney and thereupon came also a Jury to wit (Same Jury) who being elected tried and Sworn well and truly to enquire of Damages in this Suit returned "We of the Jury find for the plaintiff Seventy two dollars and thirteen cents in Damages and cost of Suit." Therefore it is considered by the Court that that the plaintiff recover the Said defendant Benjamin Kitchen his Damages aforesaid in Manner and form by the Jurors in their verdict aforesaid assessed and also his costs by him about his suit in this behalf expended and the said Defend$^t$ Benjamine in Mercy &c. - Satisfied by Benjamine Kitchens - L. Harding Att$^o$ for Pltff.

  Ordered that the overseers of the poor bind Jane Buskirk, daughter of /Blank/ Buskirk to John Callendar agreeable to Law.

---

58

  The complaint of James Blumon against Winthrop Sargent Esquire his Guardian for ill usage &c ordered to be dismissed. It appearing to the Court the same does not come properly before them.

  Ordered that the Court be adj$^d$ until tomorrow morning 9 of the clock.

---

59

       Tuesday Oct$^o$ 12$^{th}$ 1802
       The Court met according to adjournment
         Present
          Samuel Brooks
          John Henderson   Esqrs
          Ferd$^l$ L. Clairborn

(59-61)

Alexander Farrow
    against                         Refered to James Neilson and James
Ebenenezer Reese            Dick and agree that their award be
made the Judgment of the Court and the same is ordered accordingly.

The following persons were recommended to his Excellency the Governor for the purpose of obtaining Licence as Ordinary keepers in this County to wit James Dinwiddy, Capt Richard Grayton, and Leonard Pamett.

    Chas. Wilkins                 Plaintiff
       against                       In Case
    Darious Moffett              Defendant

This day came the parties by their attornies and thereupon came also a jury to wit Ezekiel Dewitt, Israel Luse, John King, Moses Moore,

---

60

Daniel Whitaker, Reubin Gibson, Abram Taylor, George Killian, Robert Throgmorton Montford Calvit, David Gibson, and Thomas Freeman who being elected tried and Sworn well and truly to try the issue joined returned, "We of the Jury find that the Defendant did assume upon himself in Manner and form as the plaintiff against him hath declared and assess his damages by occasion thereof to twenty three dollars twenty one & one half cents and costs of suit." Therefore it is considered by the Court that the plaintiff recover against the Defend$^t$ his damages aforesaid in Manner and form by the Jurors in their verdict aforesaid assessed and also his costs by him about his suit in the behalf expended and the said Defendant in Mercy &c

John Wilson against Exors. of Benjamine Monsantos Continued.

    Abner L Duncan               Plaintiff
       against                       In Case
    Abram Martin                  Defendant

The Defendant prayed an appeal Granted Bond & Secy given

---

61

An Indenture of Bargain and Sale from Daniel Ranor and wife to Archibald, and William Lewis was proved to be the act and deed of the Said Daniel and wife by the oath of John Adams witness thereto and ordered to be Recorded.

    James Carpenter             Plaintiff
       against
    John R. Wylie                Defend$^t$

This day came the parties by their attorneys and thereupon came also a Jury to wit (Same Jury) who being elected tried and sworn well and truly to try the issue Joined Returned "We of the Jury find the Defend^t guilty in the manner and form as the plaintiff in his declaration hath alledged and find for the plaintiff One Hundred dollars in Damages in damages and costs of Suit" Therefore it is Considered by the Court that the plaintiff recover against the said defendat his damages aforesaid in manner and form by the Jurors in their verdict afore's assessed and also his Costs by him about his suit in this behalf expended and the Said Defendant in Mercy &c

 Christo Lee
  against       Referred to St. James Beauverais
 Miguel Sollivellas

---

62

and Samuel Timberlake Gent and degree their award be the Judgment of the Court which award is to be returned into the Clerk's Office within six weeks and Execution to issue thereon, and the same is Ordered accordingly.

 Samuel Flower against Bonnett Truly Continued
 John Cochran      Plt.
  against       In Debt
 Abram Taylor      Deft

This day came as well the plaintiff by his Attorney as the Defendant in proper person and the said defendant acknowledged the plaintiff's action, Therefore it is Considered by the Court that the plaintiff recover against the Said defendant the sum of Eighty two dollars & Sixty six & two third cents. The Debt in the declaration mentioned and also his costs by him about his suit in this behalf expended, and the said Defendant in Mercy &c.

/Endorsed in margin/
Rec^d Satisfaction for the within Judgment
 James Wallace Att^o for the Plaintiff
Feby 16^th 1803 /End of endorsement/

---

63

Timothy Ohara against John R. Wylie Dismissed by Pltf's Attorney.
 James Barr      Plt^f
  against
 Timberlake & Hancock    Defts

This day came the parties by their attornies and the defendant Samuell Timberlake acknowledged the plaintiff's action for two hundred & Eighty one dollars fifty five & one half cents and Costs of suit.

 Christopher Lee
  against       Referred to Samuel Timberlake and Patrick
 William McWilliams    Connely with liberty to choose a third

person and agree that their award be made the Judg^t of the Court to return the same into the Clerk's office within six weeks and Execution to issue there on which is ordered accordingly.

Patrick Connelly        Plaintiff
   against
Morris Custard        Defendent

This day came the Plaintiff by his attorney

attorney and thereupon came also a Jury to wit (Same Jury) who being elected tried and Sworn well and truly to enquire of damages in this suit Returned "We of the Jury find for the plaintiff One cent in damages and Costs of Suit" Therefore it is considered by the Court that the plaintiff recover against the said defendant his damages aforesaid in Manner and form by the Jurors in their verdict aforesaid assessed and also his Costs by him about his suit in this behalf expended and the Said defendant in Mercy &c

Moses Carrol        Plt
   against
David Sherley        Deft

This day came the plaintiff by his attorney and thereupon came also a jury to wit (Same Jury) and being duly sworn to enquire of damages in this suit Returned "We of the Jury find for the plaintiff one Cent in damages and Costs of suit Therefore It is considered by the Court the plaintiff recover against the Said

defendant his damages aforesaid in Manner & form by the Jurors in their verdict aforesaid assessed and also his costs by him about his suit in the behalf expended and the said defendant in Mercy &c.

Daniel Douglass        Plt.
   against
James Green        Deft

This day came the plaintiff by his attorney & thereupon came also a Jury to wit (Same Jury) who being duly sworn well and truly to enquire of damages in this suit Returned "We of the Jury find for the plaintiff one cent in damages & Costs of Suit." Therefore it is considered by the Court that the plaintiff recover against the Said defendant his damages aforesaid in Mannor & form by the Jurors in their verdict aforesaid assessed and also his Costs by him about his Suit in this behalf expended and the defendant in Mercy &c

Rebecca McCabe
   against
Thomas Hutchens        Judgment Confessed subject to the award of James Ware and Robert Moore Exor. to be stayed on Said award until the next Term.

David Michie produced an account amounting to thirty one dollars and Eleven cents which being examined is allowed and ordered to be certified.

Charles McBride produced an account amounting to One hundred and twenty dolls. and seventy five cents which being Exam$^d$ is allowed and ordered to be Certified.

Ordered that the Court do adjourn until tomorrow Morning 9 of the clock.

---

Wednesday Oct$^o$ 13$^{th}$ 1802
The Court Met according to adjournment
        Present
          John Henderson
          Ferd$^d$ L. Clairborne Esqrs
          James Noilson

An Indenture of Bargain and Sale from Alexander Henderson to John Henderson was produce$^d$ into Court with the Certificate there endorsed and ordered to be Recorded.

Barent Stricker produced an account amounting to nineteen dollars which being examined is allowed and Ordered to be Certified.

Mary Oliver produced an account amounting to fifty two dollars and fifty Cents which being examined is allowed and ordered to be Certified.

John Holley produced an account amounting to six hundred and ninety nine dollars and fifty two & half cents which being examined is allowed and Ordered to be Certified.

---

Rebecca McCabe                  Plt
  against
Nathaniel $^T$omlinson           Deft

The defendant by his attorneys prayed an appeal to the next Superior Court of Law to be holden for the Adams District which is granted upon his giving bond with Henry Turner and Patrick Connoly his Securities in the penalty of one hundred dollars Conditioned according to Law.

Ordered that Adam Bingamin, Sutton Banks and William T. McCormick Gent inspect the State of the Jail and order such repairs as they may think necessary and report the expence of the same to the next Court.

Winsor Pipes
   Vs                                The plaintiff prayed an appeal to
John Bullon                  the next Superior Court of Law to

be holden for Adams District which is granted upon entering into Bonds with Lowis Evans and Nathaniel Tomlinson his Securities Conditioned According to law.

Anthony Daugherty produced an account amounting to forty four dollars sixty two and one half cents which being Examined is allowed and ordered to be Certified.

Sheriff of this County produced an account for Constables attendance during this Term amounting to twenty seven dollars, which being examined is allowed and ordered to be Certified.

"Ordered that the following be entered as a Rule of Court" That the Minutes be read by the Clerk on the Evening of each day and signed by the presiding Justice."

Seth Carton
Vs
Lewis Evans

Former pleadings herein withdrawn; the Defendants plead not Guilty. Joined, by Consent.

Ordered that the Clerk of this Court purchase Stationary for the use of the County and at the expence of the same and present an acct. thereof to the next Court.

An Indenture of Bargain and Sale from Ebenezer Rees to Asenoth Willis was proved by the oath of John Henderson witness thereto and ordered to be Recorded.

Evans & Overaker
vs
Ebenezer Rees

Judgment on Award and stay of Execution for thirty days And all matters in difference between, the Defendant and Lewis Evans respecting their accounts be submitted to James Andrews and Love Baker, with power to chuse an Umpire, and if their award be returned into Office in that time the balance found in favor of Said Rees shall be deducted from Said Judgment and Execution for balance, and if no award be returned in that time Execution for the whole, and said Evans shall accept of one day notice of the Meeting of Said Arbitrators and if said Evans does not attend accordingly the Arbitrators have full power to proceed exparte.

Ebenezer Rees
Vs
Nathl. Tomlinson

On motion of the Deft Dedimus awarded to examine and take the Dispoition of James Coleman in the Spanish Government.

Daniel Douglass
Vs
James Green

On motion of the Plt It is ordered that the verdict of the Jury be set aside and a new trial Granted, by Consent.

Benjamine Kitchons
Vs
James McGrath

James McGrath
Vs
Benjamin Kitchons

Referred to Love Baker and James Andrews and agree that the award be made the judgment of the Court to return the Same into the Clerk's Office within Eight Weeks and Execution to issue thereon, which is ordered accordingly

James Nielson
Vs
Benjamine Kitchens

Referred to Love Baker and James Andrews and agree that
their award be made the Judg.t of the Court to be returned into the Clerk's Office within Eight weeks and Execution to issue thereon which is ordered accordingly.

William Roe
Vs
William Brown

Appeal ordered to be dismissed.

---

72

On the motion of Joseph Newman letters of Administration on the Estate of Joshua Hames dec.d Granted him upon his entering into Bond with William Brooks and James Andrews his Securities in the penalty of five hundred Dollars Conditioned according to Law.

Ordered that Philander Smith takes the property of Elias Bronell deceased ad Colligendum Bona defuncti.

On Motion of Moses Moore Letters of Administration on the Estate of Anthony Brooks dec.d Granted upon his entering into Bond with James Dunwoody and David Johnston his securities in the penalty of One Hundred dollars Conditioned according to Law.

Elijah Craig
Vs
Miguel Sollivillas          Defendant

prayed an appeal to the Next Superior Court of Law for the District of Adams which is Granted he having

---

73

given Bond & Security agreeable to Law.

Ordered that the Court be Adj.d until the Court in Course

                    Signed
                        John Henderson.

At a County Court held for the County of Adams at the Courthouse thereof in the Town of Natchez On Monday the Sixth Day of June One thousand eight hundred and three
      Present
        Samuel Brooks
        James Nielson
        John Henderson  Esqrs
        Joseph Irvin
        John Callender

Ordered that the Platt of the prison bounds for Adams County produced by Samuel Brooks & John Henderson a committee appointed for to lay off said prison bounds be accepted and that an addition of one fourth of an acre and five perches be added to include the House of Lewis Winery and Compleat the Quantity of ten acres of Land.

John Callender absent Esqr.

On Motion of Martin McWilliams it is ordered that a Licence be granted him to keep a Tavern at his House in the County of Adams for and during the term of one year Whereupon the said Martin McWilliams, Brooks and Patrick Connally his securities entered into into an an acknowledged Bond Conditioned as the Law Directs

---

74

Richard Wheatly this day produced in Open Court a Licence from his Excellency William C. C. Claiborne Authourising him to practice as an att⁰ and Counsellor at Law who took the usual oath of Office and is admited accordingly.

| | |
|---|---|
| John Holland | Plt |
| versus | In case |
| Samuel Reynolds | Deft. |

This day came the plaintiff by Lyman Harding His Attorney & ordered that his suit be dismissed.

| | | |
|---|---|---|
| Recorded | Richard Downs | Plt. |
| | vs | In /Blank/ |
| | Joseph Lee | Deft. |

Hugh Davis and James Farrell came into Court and undertake for the defendant that in case that he be cast in the suit they will satisfy and pay the Costs and Condemnation of the Court or Surrender their Body in Execution to prison to the same or in case of failure thereof that they the said Hugh Davis and James Farrell will do it for him.

Seth Lewis. Esquire this day Produced in Open Court a Licence from his Excellency William C. C. Claiborne Authorizing him to practice as an Attorney and consulor at Law Who took the usual oath of office and is admited accordingly.

---

75

| | |
|---|---|
| Jacob Fiocundus | Plt. |
| vs | In /Blank/ |
| James Findley | Deft. |

On Motion of the Plaintiff by his Counsel it is ordered that the Suit be dismissed.

On the Motion of Jesse Greenfield and others for the View of a Road from the plantation of Charles Surget to the Town of Washington ordered that the said Jesse Greenfield, Nathaniel Tomlinson, Philander Smith, Benijah Osburn or Osman, Will Brooks, David Barney & Andrew Walker do View the most convenient way for Opaing said Road and make report thereof to the Court.

   Leo Claiborne et alias    Pltf$^s$
Recorded  Vs        In Case
   John Overaker      Deft.

This day came the plaintiff by Israel Trask his attorney and the defendant acknowledged the plaintiff's Action therefore it is considered by the Court that plaintiff recover against the Doft$^s$ Sixty four dollars and fifty four Cents the Damages adjudged & the Cost of Suit by them in this behalf expended and the Said defendant in Mercy &$^c$

   Hardress Ellis      Plt.
Recorded  Vs        In Debt
   Benjamin Carroll     Deft

This day came the parties by their attornies and thereupon came also a Jury to wit:

---

who being Elected tried and Sworn well and truly to try the Issue Joined, William Lintott, William $^C$larke, John Foster, John Callihan, David Howard, Abraham Gartney, Thomas Ford, William Eutsoll, John Martin, Ezekiel Dewitt, Joseph Strong, & John Irwin who returned the following verdict to wit "We of the Jury do find for the plaintiff one hundred and Sixteen Dollars the Debt in the Declaration mentioned with Lawful Interest from the first Day of February 1801 at the rate of five per Centum per annum with costs of suit as Damages, Therefore it is considered by the Court that the plaintiff recover against the Defendant his debt aforesaid together with his Damages in Manner and form by the Jurors aforesaid assessed & his Costs by him about his Suit in that behalf expended and the Def$^t$ in Mercy &$^c$

   William Barrow     Plt.
Recorded  Vs        In Debt  Hancock's Death
   John Hinds & Sam$^l$ Hancock Defts$^s$   Suggested

This day came the parties by their attornies and the Said Hinds surviving Def$^t$ acknowledged the plaintiffs action for one hundred and forty seven dollars amount of the note given with Interest thereon to be completed at the rate of Six per Cent$^{um}$ per annum the Interest ammounting to Eighteen Dollars eighteen cents and three fourths of a Cent in all to one hundred and sixty five Dollars and three fourth cents & Costs therefore it is considered by the Court that the plaintiff recover against the Defendant the Sum aforesaid with cost of suit &$^c$.

Daniel Ryan — Pltf
Vs — In Case
Archibald McDuffy — D

On Motion of the plaintiff by his counsel it is orderded that the suit be Dismissed.

David Kennedy — Pltf
Vs — In Case
John Bullin — Deft

it appearing to the Satisfaction of the Court the the plaintiff is Dead therefore his suit abate.

Recorded

William Barrow — Plt.
Versus — In Debt
William Price — Deft

This day came as well the plaintiff by H. L. Duncan his attorney and the Defendant in proper person and the Said Defendant acknowledged the Plaintiff's action for fifty six Dollars the amount in the note called for and Interest thereon at Six per Centum per Annum from the twenty fifth Day of December 1800 till paid which is five Dollº Intrest therefore it considered by the Court that the plaintiff recover against the Defendant the Debt Interest & Costs of suit in this behalf expended and the Said Defendant in Mercy &c.

Recorded

William Barrow — Plt.
vs — In Debt
John King — Deft

This day came the plaintiff by his Attº and the Defendant in Proper person and the said Defendant acknowledged the plaintiff's action for the Debt in the Declaration Mentioned with Interest therefore it is Considered by the Court that the plaintiff recover against the Defendant the sum of thirty five dollars the Debt in the declaration Mentioned with Interest also his costs by him about his suit in this behalf expended and the Said Deft in Mercy &c Whereupon the plaintiff acknowledged Satisfaction of thirty dollars part of the Within therefore of so much the Deft is aquited & Discharged.

Recorded

Saml P. & James Moore — Pltfs
Versus
Patrick Foley — Deft

This day came the parties by their attornies & the Deft acknowledged the plaintiff's action for Sixty four Dollars and Costs of suit therefore it is considered by the Court that the plaintiff recover against the Deft the Debt aforesaid & Costs by him about his suit in this behalf Expended.

A Report of a Road thro Captain Carter's District being Returned by the Commissioners which is in the those words to wit "Commencing at the Homochitto at Majº Abram Ellises Ferry leaving the present roads a little to the right then Crossing the same about a mile from the ferry and decending into a hollow or Valley keeping up the same a small distance then to the Right assonding a level Ridge which is kept or nearly so to a hollow about a mile below Mr. Tomlinson's and into the old Road keeping the same to Colonel Hutchins from thence by Mr. Farrar's

Plantation along the Said Road to Saint Catharine's landing from St. Catharine's landing along the Road between, the plantation of Mr. Hampton White and Mr Bonnell's keeping the said Road to the District boundary line Beginning on the above boundery line where it Crosses the Present Road which leads by Mr. William Dunbars to Maj$^r$ Ellises Forry keeping the same to the Road leading From Colonel Hutchins to Saint Catherine's Landing.

"also another commencing at the corner of Mr. Jesse Carter's pasture fence on the Road leading from St. Catherine's landing toward Mr. William Dunbar keeping along on old Road crossing Second Creek passing Mr. Carter's Gin and by where Mr. David Mitchell now lives to a plantation Commonly called Egypt belonging to Mr. Isaac Gilliard from thence to the Homochitto to a Ferry kept by Mr. Nemiah Carter or so far till it intersects the district Boundery line, Whereupon it is ordered, that the said Report be Recorded.

 James Howard adt$^{or}$     Plt.
    vs         Attach$^t$
 John Sible       Deft

Asseneth Willis being Summonsed as Garnishee and Examined and it appearing to the Satisfaction of the Court that the Said Garnishee had no Effects or Credits at the time of of Sueing [one word illegible, crossed out] Such Attachment in her hands it was ordered that the Same be Discharged.

 Samuel Timberlake    Plt
Recorded   vs        In debt
 Joseph Lee       Deft

This day came the plaintiff by Lyman Harding his attorney and the Defendant acknowledged the plaintiff's

Action, therefore it is Considered by the Court that the Plaintiff recover against the Said defendant the Sum of fifty Six Dollars and Seventy five Cents the Debt in the Declaration mentioned and also his costs by him above his suit in this behalf expended and the said Defendant in Mercy &c

The Court proceeded to appoint the following persons as overseers of the Highway for their Respective Districts To wit Captain Duncans District

                David Burney Overseer

| District | Capt$^n$ Hoggatt | Robert Childers | Overseer |
|---|---|---|---|
| do | Capt$^n$ Darby | William Foster | ditto |
| ditto | Capt$^n$ Holmes | Benjamine Holmes | ditto |
| " | Capt$^n$ Luce | Nathan Swayze | ditto |
| " | Capt$^n$ Sessions | Isaac Alexander | ditto |
| " | Capt$^n$ Carter | J. Carter | ditto |
| " | Capt$^n$ Greenleaf | John Martin | ditto |
| " | Capt$^n$ Guice | Capt$^n$ Guice | ditto |
| " | Philander Smith | Jesse Greenfield | ditto |

Ordered that the afore mentioned overseers do Summons the hands in each of the Districts to work thereon when necessarily Required and keep the same in Repair. The Court ordered that the following persons be appointed as Overseers of the poor to wit

| Capt$^n$ Duncan | District | David Gibson | Overseer |
|---|---|---|---|
| " Hoggatts | ditto | Anthony Hoggatt | ditto |
| " Darby | ditto | Robert Dunbar | ditto |

| | | | |
|---|---|---|---|
| Capt$^n$ Holmes | ditto | John Irwin | ditto |
| " Luce | ditto | Caleb King | ditto |
| " Sessions | ditto | Joseph Howard | ditto |
| " Carter | ditto | Jn$^o$ H. White | ditto |
| " Greenlief | ditto | Jn$^o$ Bowls | ditto |
| " S$^d$ Smith | ditto | Jesse Greenfield | ditto |
| " Guice | ditto | Joseph Ford | ditto |

The above app is ordered to be Certified.

---

Ordered that the Several Tavern Keepers within this County take and Receive for the following Articles To Wit

| | |
|---|---|
| For Breakfast | .37½ |
| " Dinner | .50 |
| " Supper | .37½ |
| " Lodging | .25 |
| " Feeding horse | .25 |
| " 24 Hours at Hay & Fodder | .75 |
| " 1 night ditto | .50 |
| " 1 Bottle Maderia | 2.00 |
| " Best Boardeaux do | 1.50 |
| " Com$^n$ Claret pt Bottle | 1.00 |
| " ½ pint Coneack Brandy | .50 |
| " ½ pint Holland Gin | .50 |
| " 1 Bottle Porter | 1.00 |
| " ½ pt Country Gin | .25 |
| " ½ do Jamaica Spirits | .50 |
| " ½ pt Whiskey | .12½ |
| " ½ pt Peach Brandy | .18-3/4 |
| " 1 Quart Cider | .18-3/4 |

The prices on the above Rates the Tavern Keepers within this County may receive & not more.

Ebenezer Rees    Plt
 vs       In /Blank/
Authur Cobb    Deft

On the Motion of the Defendant by his Attorney who prays that the Judgment obtained against him may be Set aside arrested and the trial thereof is defered for the last day of the Court.

Court adjourned until tomorrow morning at nine o'clock

---

The Court agreeable to adjournment met
  Present
   Samuel Brooks
   John Henderson  Esquires
   James Neilson

Thomas Moore Esqr having produced a Licence from his Excellency William C. C. Claiborne to practice as an attorney and Counseller at Law in the Several Counties within this territory whereupon he took the oath by Law Required and is admitted accordingly.

Recorded

| | | |
|---|---|---|
| Ann Martin | Plt | |
| vs | In Case | |
| Ezekiel Dewitt | Deft | |

This day came the parties by their attornies and agree that the pleadings of this cause be made up in form and plead a General Replication and Joinder and thereupon came also a Jury To wit William Lintot, William Clark, John Martin, David Greenleaf, John Irwin, William Hutsell, John Calhoun, Thomas Ford, Abram Galtney, Joseph Strong, David Howard and John Mitchell who being elected tried and Sworn to try the issue Joined upon their oath do say that the Defendant is not Guilty in Manner and form as the Plaintiff hath Declared, therefore it is Considered by the Court that the defendant go hence without Day and Recover against the Plaintiff his Costs by her about his suit in this behalf expended and that the plaintiff with her false Clamour be in Mercy &c

William Cochran being Summonsed to serve on a Petit Jury & failing to attend, tho Solemnly Called, it is ordered by the Court for his Contempt therein that he be fined two dollars & Costs & that he may be taken &c

---

83

| | |
|---|---|
| Moores Extors | Plt |
| Vs | In /Blank/ |
| Donalson & Wife | Defts |

Charles King who was Special Bail in this Action Surrendered the Bodies of the Defendant in Open Court in Discharge of his Recognizance and undertaking & and thereupon George Williams comes into Court & undertakes for the Defendants that in Case they be cast in the suit, that he will Satisfy and pay the condemnation of the Court or render his body in Execution to prison for the same or in case of failure he the said George will do it for them

| | |
|---|---|
| King and Sacket | Pltfs |
| Vs | In D |
| Samuel Ashlook | Deft |

Charles King who was special Bail in this action Surrendered the Bodies of the Defendant in Court in Discharge of his recognizance and undertaking Joseph Newman and Thomas Regan came into Court and undertakes for the Defendant that in Case he shall be cast in this suit they Shall Satisfy and pay the costs of Condemnation of the Court or render their his bodies to prison in Execution for the same or in Case of failure thereof that they the said Joseph & Thomas will do it for him.

Adam Tooley this day presented in Court an acct. of The Marks and Brands used in Designating his live Stock according to Law, which is ordered to be Recorded.

Manuel Tarsadu        Plt
   Vs                 In /Blank/
Daniel Douglass       Deft

This day came the plaintiff by his attorney and the Defendant in proper person and the Said defendant acknowledges the Plaintiff's action Therefore it is Considered by the Court that the Plaintiff Recover against the Said Defendant the Sum of three hundred and twenty Seven Dollars & Damages to be assessed by Abija Hunt & Henry James and the award to be Returned in the office and Execution Stayed Six Weeks From this time Award Rec$^d$ by Consent for 77 Dollars 97 cents Damg$^s$ making in the whole four hundred & five Dollars Twenty two cents & cost of Suit.

Ann Martin            Plt
   Vs                 In /Blank/
Ezekiel Dewitt        Deft

This day came the Plaintiff by his attorney and prayed an appeal to the next Superior Court which is Granted Upon her entering into an acknowledged Bond with William B. Smith and John Eldergile his securities Conditioned according to Law.

Jesse Hamilton        Plt
   Vs                 Attachment
Cyrus Hamilton        Deft

Frederick Ward as Garnishee in The above Suit appeared in Court declared on oath that he had cotton Receipts in his hand which he purchased from the Defendant amounting to two hundred Dollars therefore Judgment is entered against the Garnishee for the Said two hundred dollars provided that the Cotton is good, if not Good the Said Cotton to be liable to discharge the Said Judgment.

---

On Motion of Francis Keller it is Ordered that a Licence be granted him to keep a Tavern on this County at his House during the Term of one year upon his entering into and acknowledged bond with Ja$^s$ Hoggatt his security Conditioned according to law.

Garrett Pendergrass           Plt
   Vs                         In Case
Martin Hinderlider Ad$^m$     Deft

This day came the parties by their attornies and agree to Submit all matters in Difference between them to the final determination of John Henderson Esquire and his award to be made the Judgement of the Court to return the same in the Clerk's office and Execution to Issue thereon.

The Commissioners appointed to View and mark the most convenient way for publick Road thro Capt Carter's District motioned for the establishment thereof the Consideration which is Suspended until Wednesday next.

              Jonathan Davis            Plt
Recorded         Vs                     In debt
              Benj$^m$ Kitchens & Smith Deft

This day came the Plaintiff by his attorney and the Defendant in Proper Person and the Said Defendant acknowledges the plaintiffs action Therefore it is considered by the Court that the Plaintiff recover against the Said the Sum of thirty two dollars the Debt in the Declaration mentioned and his Costs by him about his Suit in in this behalf expended and the Defendant in Mercy &c

|  |  |  |
|---|---|---|
| begin | David Ferguson & Woolley | Pltff$^s$ |
|  | & | In Case |
| Recorded | Hardress Ellis | Def$^t$ |

This day came the plaintiffs by their attorney and the Def$^t$ in proper person and acknowledges the Plaintiff's action therefore it is Considered by the Court that the Plaintiff recover against the said defendant the Sum of thirty Six Dollars and twenty five Cents & also his costs by him in this behalf expended and the Defendant in Mercy &c and the plaintiff agrees to Stay Execution three months.

|  |  |  |
|---|---|---|
|  | Lowis Burnet | Plt |
| Recd | Vs | In Case |
|  | Joseph Strikland | Def$^t$ |

This day came the Plaintiff by his Attorney and the Def$^t$ in proper Person and the Said Defendant acknowledges the plaintiff's action therefore it is Considered by the Court that the plaintiff recover against the Defendant the sum of Sixty five Dollars and also his Costs by him about his suit in this behalf expended and the Said Defendant in Mercy &c and the plaintiff agrees to stay execution three months.

Edward Maloney     Plt
Vs     In Case
Michael Moore     Deft

Appearing to the satisfaction of the Court that the Defendant is dead therefore this Suit abates.

Robert Moore & Co.     Plt
versus     In
Richard Horton     Deft

Israel Smith comes into Court and undertakes for the Defendant that in Case he should be cast in this suit he shall Satisfy & pay the Costs and condemnation of the Court or Render his Body to prison in Execution for the Same or in case of failure thereof that he the Said Israel will do it for him

Moses Saxon     Plt
Versus     In Trespass Vi et Armis
John F. Carmicheal     Deft

On the Motion of the plaintiff by his Counsel it is ordered that this suit be dismissed.

|  |  |  |
|---|---|---|
|  | Arthur Strother | Plt |
| Recorded | Vers | In Case |
|  | Patrick Foley | Deft |

This day came the plaintiff by his attorney and the Defendant in proper
person and the Said defendant acknowledges the plaintiff's action for fifty
three dollars and ninety Two cents therefore it is considered by the Court
the Plaintiff recover against the Said Defendant the said Sum mentioned
and also his Costs by him about his Suit in the behalf expended and the
Said Defendant in Mercy &c & the plaintiff agrees to to Stay execution Six
weeks.

| | |
|---|---|
| Lewis Sojourner | Plt |
| Vs | In Case |
| John Mitchell | Deft |

On Motion of the plaintiff by his Counsel Ordered that the suit be dismissed.

Court adjourned.

---

Court met according to adjournment
Wednesday 8th of June one thousand
eight hundred & three
Present
Saml Brooks
Joseph Sessions   Esquires
John Callendar
Saml Boyd

| | |
|---|---|
| Richard May | Plt |
| Versus | In Case |
| Martin Hinderlider Ad<sup>tor</sup> | Def |

This Day came the parties by their attornies and thereupon came also a
Jury to wit William Lintott, William Clarke, John Martin, David Greenlief. John Irwin, William Hutsell, John Calliham, Thomas Ford, Abram
Gaultney, Joseph Strong, John Foster & Ezekiel Dewitt who being elected
tried & Sworn the truth to Speak upon the Issue Joined upon their oath
do Say "that the Deceased John David Upon in his life time did assume
in Manner and form or in the Declaration mentioned therefore find for
the Plaintiff Sixty Dollars damages & Cost of Suit". Therefore it is
considered by the Court that the plaintiff Recover the Said defendant
his damages aforesaid in Manner and form by the Jurors in their Verdict
aforesaid assessed and also his costs by him about his suit in this behalf expended and the Defendant in Mercy &c

| | |
|---|---|
| William Murray | Plt |
| Vs | Atta |
| Thomas Hutchins | Deft |

On motion leave to amend the Return of the attachment by adding the
date of the Levying

---

| | | |
|---|---|---|
| | Ezekiel Dewitt | Plt |
| Recorded | vs | In Debt |
| | Simon Spring | Deft |

(89-90)

Recorded

This day came the parties by their Attornies, and Thereupon came a Jury to wit, William Lintott, William Clark, John Martin, David Greenlief, John Irwin, William Hutsell, John Calliham, Thomas Ford, Abram Gaultney, Joseph Strong, John Foster ~~Ezekiel Bewitt~~ Charles King who being elected tried and Sworn well and truly to try the Issue Joined upon their oath do say that the Defendant ~~is guilty in~~ manner and form as the plaintiff in his declaration hath declared and we do assess the plaintiff damages by occasion thereof the debt in the Declaration mentioned with interest thereon at the rate of five per centum per annum till paid also his costs by him about his Suit in this behalf expended therefore it is considered by the Court that the plaintiff recover against the Said Defendant his debt and interest aforesaid in manner and form by the Jurors in their verdict aforesaid assessed and also his costs by him about his Suit in this behalf expended and the Said defendant in Mercy &c

|  |  |  |
|---|---|---|
| Recorded | Ebenezer Snow vs Elisha Fisher | Plt In Case Deft |

This day came the plaintiff by his attorney and the Defendant in Proper person and the Said defendant acknowledges the plaintiff's action Therefore it is considered by the Court that the plaintiff recover against the said Defendant twenty one Dollars and his costs by him about his suit in this behalf expended.

---

90

|  | Churchwell Vs Moore | Plaintiff In /Blank/ Defendant |
|---|---|---|

On Motion Plea of non Asumpsit to the Court withdrawn & cause continued.

|  | Edwin L. Harris Vs Thomas & William Cochran, | Plt In /Blank/ Deft | Recd the amount of Judgt Bon Jn̄ Seaman clk |
|---|---|---|---|
| Recd |  |  |  |
| 92 |  |  |  |
| 35 |  |  |  |
| 57 |  |  |  |

This day came the plaintiff by his attorney and the Defendt in Proper Person and the said defendant acknowledges the plaintiff's action Therefore it is considered by the Court that the plaintiff recover against the Said Defendant The Sum of eighty five dollars and Seven Dollars Damages and his Costs by them about his suit in this behalf expended and the said defendant in Mercy &c & Costs $8.90 Debt, damages & costs paid clerk Sept 27th 1803.

Debt 85
Dam 7
Cost 8.90
100.00
44.60
56.30
8.90
47.40

|  | Phebe Cochran | Pltf |  |
|---|---|---|---|
|  | Vs | In /Blank/ | Recd the amt of |
|  | Rebekah McCabe | Def^t | Judg^t B. Seamans |
| Award | 35 |  | Referred to |
| Cost | 9.60 |  | William T McCammack |
|  | 44.60 | | |

and am^t to be deducted from the above Judgment Harris vs Cochran award returned for thirty five dollars to be deducted above Judg^t & Costs $9.60 Debt & cost deducted from forging Judg^t & Costs paid Sept 27^th 1803.

|  | Davis Ferguson & Wooley | Plaintiffs |
|---|---|---|
| Recorded | vs | In Case |
|  | James Findley | Defendant |

This day came the plaintiff by his attorney and the Defendant in Proper person and the Said Defendant acknowledged the plaintiff's action therefore it is considered by the Court that the plaintiffs recover against the Said defendant the Sum of one hundred and forty one Dollars and forty four cents and his costs by him above his suit in this behalf expended and the Deft in Mercy &^c

---

91

|  | David Ferguson & Woolley | Plaintiffs |
|---|---|---|
|  | Vs | In /Blank/ |
|  | Patrick Connelly | Defendant |

Refered to John Farrell and John Henderson Esquires whose award to be Returned in the Clerk's office in Six weeks and made the Judgment of the Court and Exeution to Issue thereon.

|  | David Ferguson & Woolley | Plaintiffs |
|---|---|---|
| Recorded | Vs | In Case |
|  | James Findley & P. Connelly | Defendants |

This day came the plaintiff by his attorney and the Defendant in pro person and the Said Defendant acknowledges the plaintiff's action therefore it is considered by the Court that the plaintiffs Recover against the Said Defendant fifty nine Dollars and Seventy Six cents and also his costs by him about his Suit in this behalf expended and the said Defendant in Mercy &^c

|  | ~~Same vs Findley~~ | ~~Dft~~ | ~~As above for the Debt & cents~~ |
|---|---|---|---|
|  | Leonard Claiborne | Plaintiff |  |
| Recorded | Vs | In Case |  |
|  | Benjamine Kitchens | Defendant | Refered to Peter A. |

Vandorn & and Love Baker award to be Returned into the Clerk's office to be made the final Determination of the Court and Execution thereon after the exporation of Six Weeks.

|  | John Scott | Plaintiff |
|---|---|---|
|  | Vs | In Case |
|  | John Wilson | Defendant |

This suit abates on the Death of the plaintiff

Patrick Connally   Plaintiff
Vs   In [Blank]
Daniel Douglass   Defendant

The parties agree to Refer the Matters in Difference to James Farrell and John Henderson.

William Muncey   Plt
Vs   In [Blank]
Benjamine Kitchens   Deft

The parties agree to stay all further proceedings on the above Suit Twelve Months.

William Brocher Ad$^{tor}$   Plaintiff
Versus   In Case
Archabald Palmer   Defend$^t$

On Motion of the plaintiff by his Counsel, it is ordered that this Suit be Dismissed.

   St James Beauvier   Plaintiff
Recorded    V   In Debt
   James Bosley   Defendant

This day came the plaintiff by their Attorney and the Deft. in proper person and the Said Defendant acknowledges the plaintiff's action therefore it is Considered by the Court that the Plaintiff recover against the Said Defendant the Sum of thirty eight Dollars and twenty nine cents also his costs by him about his suit in this behalf expended and the Said Defendant in Mercy &c

Ordered that Court adjourn till tomorrow morning nine O'Clock.

---

93

       Thursday the Ninth the Court
       Met according to adjournment
        Sam$^l$ Brooks
        John Callender   Esquires
        Sam$^l$ Boyd

   Pheba Martin   Plaintiff
Recorded    Vs   In Case
   John Wells   Defendant

This day came the parties by their attornies & leave granted to withdraw plea of General Issue and leave to file Justification claiming the Pltf as the Property of the Defendants Slave for life and Replications with Issue thereon Jury to try the Same to wit: William Lintot, William Clark, and John Martin, David Greenlief John Irwin, William Hutsell and John Calliham, Thomas Ford, Abraham Gaultney, John Foster, Ezekiel Dewitt & Anthony Calvit, Returned To of the Jury find for the Plt and that the Defendant is Guilty of the Trespass and false Imprisonment as charged in the Declaration and assess her Damages to one cent with cost of Suit.

Motion for new trial.

Samm$^l$ Flower   Plaintiff
Vs   In Case
Nathaniel Tomlinson   Defendant   Rule of Reference

The parties agree to Refer all matters in difference between them to the

final Determination of Robert Cochran and James Farrell: Their award to
be returned in this office in Six weeks [one word illegible, crossed out]
made the Judgment of the Court and entered thereon as of this term and
Execution to Issue accordingly.

94

| | |
|---|---|
| Abjah Hunt & Co. | Plaintiff |
| Vs | In Case |
| Patrick Connelly | Defendant |

This day came the Plaintiffs by their Attorney and the Defendant in proper
person and the Said Defendant acknowledges the Plaintiffs' action therefore it is considered by the Court that the plaintiff recover against the
Said Defendant the sum of one hundred and fifty eight Dollars and forty
Two cents and also their Costs by him about their Suit in this behalf Expended and the Said Deft in Mercy &c. The Plaintiffs agree to Stay execution of this Judgment till first of September next.

| | |
|---|---|
| Charles Wilkins | Plaintiff |
| Vs | In Case |
| John Saxon | Defendant |

This day came the Plaintiff by his Attorney and the Defendant in proper
person and the Said Defendant agrees to Satisfy and pay the Costs in the
above suit therefore it is considered by the court that the plaintiff Recover against the Said Defendant his costs by him about his suit in this
behalf expended & the Said Deft in Mercy &c

On Motion of James Dunlap, Attorney for the United States to appoint
some Day for the hearing The Causes of the Said States Ordered that the
Said motion be laid over till Thursday next.

95

| | |
|---|---|
| Daniel McMullen | Plaintiff |
| versus | In Case |
| George Carmick | Defendant |

This day came the parties by their Attornies and Thereupon came also a
Jury to wit William Lintot, William Clarke, John Martin, David Greenleaf,
John Irwin, William Hutsell, John Callihan, Thomas Ford, Abraham Gaultney
John Foster, Ezekiel Dewitt & Stephen Stephenson who being elected tried
and Sworn well and truly to try the Issue Joined Returned, "We of the Jury
found that the Defendant did assume in Manner and form as the plaintiff
in his Declaration hath complained against and assess his damages to thirty
six Dollars and costs of suit, Therefore it is Considered by the Court that
the plaintiff recover ags the Said Defendant his damages aforesaid in manner and form by the Juriors in their verdict aforesaid assessed and also
his costs by him about his Suit in this behalf expended and the Said Defendant in Mercy &c

| | |
|---|---|
| James Beauvies | Plaintiff |
| Vs | In Debt |
| Rebecca McCabe | Defendant |

This day came the parties by their Attornies and there upon came also a
Jury to wit William Lintot, William Clark, John Martin, David Greenleaf
John Irwin, W^m Hutsell, John Calliham, Thomas Ford, Abraham Gaultney
John Foster, Ezekiel and Stephen Stephenson by Consent of the parties
the Jurors from returning their verdict and withdrawn and the Said Defendant relinquishing her former plea acknowledges the plaintiffs action therefore it is considered by the Court that the plaintiff

recover against the Said Defendant the Sum of One hundred and sixty two
Dollars and twenty five cents also their Costs by her about their Suit in
this behalf expended and the said Defendant in Mercy &c

  Henry Turner    Plt
    Vs       In Case
  William Silkreg   Deft

This day came the plaintiff by his attorney and the Defendant in proper
person and the Said Defendant acknowledges the plaintiff's action therefore it is considered by the Court that ~~that~~ the plaintiff recover against
the said Defendant the sum of one hundred and twenty seven Dollars and
also his costs by him about his Suit in this behalf expended and the Said
Defendant in Mercy &c

  Thompson     Pltf
    Vs       Attach^d
  Richey      Deft

Peter [Blank] and William [Blank] come into Court and undertake for the
Defendant that in case he shall be Cast in this Suit they will Satisfy and
pay the Costs and condemnation of the Court or Surrender their Bodies in
Execution to prison for the Same or in Case of failure thereof that they
the Said Peter and William will do it for him.

  John Scott     Plt
    vs       In [Blank]
  John Willson    Deft

The above suit abates on the Death of the Pltff.

  Jacob Yirzer    Plaintiff
    vs       In Case
  Jacob Ficundas   Defendant

This day came the Defendant by his attorney and the plaintiff being
Solemnly called came not, therefore it is considered by the Court that
the plaintiff be nonsuited and that the Defendant go hence without Day
and Recover against the plaintiff his Costs by him about his Suit in this
behalf expended.

     Daniel Clarke    Plaintiff
Recorded   Vs       In Case    Hancock's Death
     Regan Timberlake & Hancock  Defendants  Suggested

This day came the parties by their attornies and thereupon came also a Jury to wit William Lintot, William Clarke, John Martin, David Greenleaf, John Irwin, William Hutsell, John Calliham, Thomas Ford, Abraham Gaultney, John Foster, Ezekiel Dewitt & Anthony Calvet, who being elected tried and Sworn the Truth to Speak upon the Issue Joined Upon their oaths do Say that the Defendant is Guilty in manner and form as the plaintiff against them hath Declared in his Declaration & we do assess the plaintiff Damages by occasion thereof to one hundred and fifty six Dollars and fifty Cents and also his Costs by him about his Suit in this behalf expended and the Said Defendant in Mercy &c & the plaintiff agrees to Stay execution till fourth Sep$^t$ next.

---

98

Mr. John Burnett having produced a Licence from his Excellency William C. C. Claiborne to practice as an attorney & Counsellor at Law whereupon he took the oath by law Required and was admitted accodingly.

Court adjourned till tomorrow morning 9 O'clock.

Friday 10$^{th}$ the Court According to Ad$^t$ met

Present
Sam$^l$ Brooks
Abner Green   Esquires
Caleb King

Reese
Vs
Tomlinson
Same Ex$^{tors}$
&
Same
Same Surviving Partners
Vs
Same

Refered to James Wallace & E. H. Bradish Esquires whose award to be returned into the Clerk's Office in Six Weeks or Judgment to be entered against the Defendant on failure on his part to attend and on failure of the Plaintiffs likewise, the

Suit to be Dismissed with costs, the parties to meet on Saturday the eighteenth instant.

Thomas Tyler                Plaintiff
Vs                          In Case
Anthony Calvet              Defendant

This day came the Plaintiff by his attorney and the Defendant in proper person and the Said Defendant acknowledges the plaintiffs action therefore it is considered by the Court that the plaintiff recover against the Said Defendant the Sum of one hundred and forty three Dollars and fifty five cents and also his costs by him about his Suit in this behalf expended and the Said Defendant in Mercy &c & the plaintiff agrees to Stay execution till first Sept.

| | |
|---|---|
| Manuel Loopez | Plaintiff |
| vs | In Case |
| Christopher Lee | Defendant |

This day came the plaintiff by his Attorney and the Defendant in proper person and the Said Defendant acknowledges the plaintiffs action therefore it is considered by the Court that the plaintiff recover against the said Defendant the Sum of thirty Seven Dollars and Seventy five Cents and also his Costs by him about his suit in this behalf expended and the Plaintiff agrees to Stay Execution of this Judgment till first of September next.

On the Motion of Martha Reed it is Ordered that a Licence be granted her to keep a tavern at her house in this County for and during the term of one year from the date hereof and until the next Succeeding County Court thereafter She having entered into and acknowledged Bond with Prosper King and John Bowls his Securities Cont$^d$ as the Law Directs.

| | |
|---|---|
| Abijah Hunt Ad$^{tor}$ | Plaintiff |
| vs | In Case |
| Patrick Connolly | Defendant |

This day came the plaintiff by his Attorney and the Defendant in proper person and the Said Defendant acknowledges the plaintiffs action therefore it is considered by the Court that the plaintiff recover against the the Said Defendant the Sum of Sixty Seven Dollars and fifty eight cents and also his Costs by him about his Suit in this behalf expended and the Said Defendant in Mercy &$^c$ the plaintiff agrees to Stay the Execution of the Judgment two months.

---

| | |
|---|---|
| Flower | Plaintiff |
| vs | |
| Wilson Dec$^d$ | Defendant |

Ordered that a Scire facias issue against James Farrell and Richard King Executors of the Said Wilson Deceased to show cause ~~cause~~ if any they can, why this Suit Should not be Revived against them as Executors aforesaid.

| | |
|---|---|
| Bartholomus Thamburgh | Plaintiff |
| vs | In Case |
| Garrot E. Pendergrast | Defendant |

This day came the parties by their Attornies and thereupon came also a Jury to wit: William Lintot, William Clarke, John Martin, John Irwin, William Hutsell John Calliham, Thomas Ford, John Foster, Ezekiel Dewitt, Stephen Stephenson, William Cochran, and Bennet Truly who being elected tried and Sworn well and truly to try the Issue Joined upon their oath do say "We of the Jury find for the plaintiff two hundred and forty Six Dollars and thirty four cents with cost of Suit," therefore it is considered by the Court that the plaintiff recover against the Said Defendant his Sum aforesaid in Manner & form by the Jurors in their verdict aforesaid assessed and also his Costs by him about his Suit in this behalf expended and the said Defendant in Mercy &$^c$

                    Abijah Hunt                    Plaintiff
Recorded            Vs                             In Case
                    Patrick Connelly               Defendant

This day came the plaintiff by his attorney and the Defendant in proper
person and the Defendant acknowledges the plaintiff's action therefore
it is considered by the court that the plaintiff recover against the said
Defendant the Sum of one hundred and two dollars and thirty Cents and also
his Costs by him about his Suit in this behalf expended and the plaintiff
agrees to Stay the Execution of this Judgment until the first Sept next.

                    Rebecca McCabe                 Plaintiff
                    versus                         In Case
                    Thomas Hutchens                Defendant

This day came the plaintiff by his attorney and it appearing the former
Rule of Reference not being Complied with, it is ordered the same be discharged and the Defendant in his proper person comes into Court and acknowledges the plaintiff's action therefore it is considered by the Court
that the plaintiff recover against the Said Defendant the Sum of two hundred and forty two Dollars and also his Costs by him about his Suit in this
behalf expended and the plaintiff.

                    Abram Martin                   Plaintiff
Recorded            vs                             In Debt
                    John Morris                    Defendant

This day came the plaintiff by his attorney and the Defendant in proper
person and the Said Defendant acknowledges the plaintiff's action, therefore it is considered by the Court that the plaintiff recover against the
Said Defendant the sum of Sixty Dollars the Debt in the Declaration mentioned
and nine Dollars and Sixty Cents Damages also his Costs by him about his Suit
in this behalf expended and the Said Defendant in Mercy &c . This Judg$^t$
Subject to any Defalcation which may be made before the Clerk within two
Months.

                    Abijah Hunt                    Plaintiff
Recorded            vs                             In Case
                    Patrick Connelly & Patrick Foley, Defendant

This day came the plaintiff by his attorney and the Defendants in proper
persons and the Said Defendants acknowledges the plaintiffs action therefore it is considered by the Court that the plaintiff recover against the
Said Defendant the Sum of one hundred and twenty two Dollars and ten Cents
also his Costs by them about his Suit in this behalf Expended and the Said
Defendant in Mercy &c, & agree to stay execution of this Judgment till first
of Sep$^t$ next.

                    William Bruin                  Plaintiff
                    Vs                             In Case
                    Patrick Foley                  Defendant

This day came the plaintiff by his attorney and the Deft in proper person
and the Said Defendant acknowledges the plaintiff's action therefore it is
considered by the Court

that the plaintiff recover against the Said Defendant the Sum of forty three dollars and Eighty cents and also his Costs by him about his Suit in this behalf Expended and the said Defendant in Mercy &c and agree to Stay execution till the first of Sept next.

    Daniel Clark    Plaintiff
Recorded  Vs        In Case
    Samuel Timberlake   Def$^{ndt}$

This day came the plaintiff by his Attorney and the Defendant in his proper person and the Said defendant acknowledges the plaintiff's action therefore it is considered by the Court that the plaintiff recover against the Said Defendant the Sum of Eighty two Dollars and fifty and also his Costs by him about his suit in this behalf Expended and the said Defendant in Mercy &c and agree to stay execution of the Judgment till first of September next.

    David Ferguson & Woolley  Ptffs
    vs         In Case
    William Mulhallon    Deft

This day came the plaintiff by his attorney and the Deft in proper person and the Said Defendant acknowledges the plaintiff's action, therefore it is Considered by the Court that the plaintiff recover against the Said Defendant the Sum of thirty Seven Dollars and twenty nine cents and also their Costs by him about his Suit in this behalf expended and the Said Defendant in Mercy &c and agree Stay of execution until the first of September next.

---

    Abijah Hunt Ad$^{tor}$    Plaintiff
Recorded  Vs        in Case
    Sam$^{l}$ Timberlake    Defendant

This day came the plaintiff by his attorney and the Defendant in proper person and the Said Defendant acknowledges the plaintiff's action therefore it is considered by the Court that the plaintiff recover against the Said Defendant the Sum of Eighty Dollars and ten cents and also his Costs by him about his Suit in this behalf Expended and the Said Defendants in Mercy &c and agree to Stay Execution of this judgment until September next.

    Abijah Hunt Ad$^{tor}$    Plaintiff
    Vs         In Case
    Samuel Timberlake & Hancock  Defendant

This day came the plaintiff by his Attorney and the Defendant in proper person and the Said Defendant acknowledges the plaintiffs action therefore it is considered by the Court that the plaintiff recover against the Said Deft the Sum of Eighty five Dollars and also his Costs by him about his Suit in this behalf expended and the Said Deft in Mercy &c and agree to stay the execution of this Judg$^{t}$ until next court.

    William Kenner    Plaintiff
    vs         In Case
    Elias Fisher     Defendant

This day came the plaintiff by his attorney and the Defendant in proper person and the Said defendant acknowledges the plaintiffs action therefore it is considered by the Court that the plaintiff recover against the Defendant the Sum of Eighty Eight Dollars and thirty Six Cents also his Costs by him about his Suit in this behalf expended and the Said Defendant in Mercy &c and agree to stay execution of this Judgt until Sept next.

|  |  |
|---|---|
| The Same | Plaintiff |
| vs | In Case |
| John Bosley | Defendant |

This day came the plaintiff by his Attorney and the Defendant in proper person and the Said Defendant acknowledges the plaintiff's action therefore it is considered by the Court that the plaintiff recover against the Said Defendant the Sum of thirty one Dollars Sixty three cents and also his costs by him about his Suit in this behalf expended and the said Defendant in Mercy &c and agree to Stay execution of this Judgment until first of September next.

|  |  |  |
|---|---|---|
|  | Robert Glass | Plaintiff |
| Recorded | Vs | in Debt |
|  | Michael Lougham | Defendant |

This day came the plaintiff by his Attorneys and the Defendant in proper person and the Said Defendant acknowledges the plaintiff's action therefore it is Considered by the Court that the plaintiff recover against the Said Defendant the Sum of one hundred and forty five Dollars & Seventy five cents as the Debt in the Declaration mentioned and ten Dollars & Sixty eight cents Damages and also his Costs by him about his Suit in this behalf expended and the Said Defendant in Mercy &c and agree to stay execution of this Judgment until first of Sept next. - Costs $10.

|  |  |
|---|---|
| James Beauvies & Co. | Plaintiff |
| vs | On Attachment |
| David Barbour | Defendant |

This day came the plaintiff by his attorney and the Sheriff having made return of the Said attachment in these words, "18$^{th}$ of Jan$^{ry}$ 1803 agreeable to the within attachment I proceeded to the Dwelling house of St James Beauvies and Levied the within on one new Broad Cloth Coat and a pair Blue Cashmere Pantaloons and one black Sattin Vest, all new, which Clothing I now have in My possession, and the Defendant failing to appear and replevy the Same therefore it is ordered that Sheriff do make Sale of the attached effects and the money arising therefrom to be Deposited in the hands of the Clerk until the final determination of this Suit."

|  |  |
|---|---|
| Benjamine Stokes | Plaintiff |
| vs | in Case |
| Winthrop Sargent | Defendant |

This day came the parties by their attornies and thereupon came also a Jury to wit, Thomas Regan, William Clarke, John Martin, John Irwin, William Hutsell, John Calliham, Thomas Ford, John Foster, Ezekiel Dewitt,

Stephen Stephenson, William Cochram, & Bennet Truly who being elected tried and Sworn well and truly to try the Issue Joined upon their oath do say that the Defendant is Guilty in manner and form as the plaintiff in his Declaration hath complained and do assess the plaintiffs Damages by occasion thereof to thirty five Dollars and twenty five cents also his Costs by him about his Suit in this behalf expended and the said Defendant in Mercy &$^c$

---

Court adjourned eight o'clock the following Day June the eleventh One thousand eight hundred and three

    Present
     Sam$^l$ Brooks
     Abner Green    Esquires
     John Callender

Stacpoole
vs
Phipps

George Cochran and Melling Woolley Ex$^{tors}$ of Morris Stacpoole Deceased by Ebenezer Bradish their attorney came into Court and made themselves plaintiff in the Suit of Said Stacpoole against Phipps.

  John O'Connor      Plaintiff
Recorded   vs         In Case
  Alexander Farrar     Defendant

This day came the plaintiff by his attorney and the Defendant in proper person and the Said Defendant acknowledges the plaintiff's action, therefore it is considered by the Court that the plaintiff recover against the Said defendant the sum of one hundred and fourteen Dollars and also his costs by him about his suit in this behalf expended and the Said Defendant in Mercy &$^c$ and agree to Stay execution of this Judgment until the first of September next.

---

Young        Peter Walker comes into Court and
vs         undertakes for the Defendants that
Atchison       in case they be cast in this Suit
Barland        that he that he will Satisfy and
vs         pay the Costs and Condemnation of
Same         the Court or Surrender his body to
          prison in Execution for the same or
in Case of failure thereof That he the Said Peter will do it for him.

  William Loan      Plaintiff
  vs         Trover & Conversion
  Patrick Connolly     Defendant

This day came the parties by their attornies and thereupon came also a Jury to wit, William Clarke, John Martin, John Irwin, William Rutsell, John Callihan, Thomas Ford, John Faster, Ezekel Dewitt, Stephen Stephenson, William Cochran & Nathaniel Cochran who being elected tried and Sworn well and truly to try the Issue Joined upon their oath do Say that the Defendant is not guilty in Manner & form as the plaintiff in his Declaration hath complained therefore it is considered by the Court that the plaintiff take nothing for his bill but for his false Clameur be in Mercy &c and that the Defendant go thereof without Day and recover against the plaintiff his Costs by him about his Defence in this behalf expended.

109

| | |
|---|---|
| John O'Connor | Plaintiff |
| vs | In Case |
| John Calvet | Defendant |

This day came the plaintiff by his attorney and the said Defendant in proper person and the Said Deft acknowledges the plaintiff's action therefore it is considered by the Court that the plaintiff recover against the Said Defendant the Sum of ninety Seven Dollars and fifty one Cents and also his Costs by him about his Suit in this behalf expended and the Said Defendant in Mercy &c and agree to Stay execution of this Judgment until the first of September next.

| | |
|---|---|
| The Same Recorded | Plaintiff |
| vs | In Case |
| William Fletcher | Defendant |

This day came the plaintiff by his attorney and the Defendant in proper person and the said Defendant acknowledges the plaintiff's action therefore it is considered by the Court that the plaintiff recover against the Said Defendant the sum of one hundred and forty Six Dollars and ninety three cents and also his Costs by him about his Suit in this behalf expended and the Said Defendant in Mercy &c and the Plt agree to Stay the Execution of this Judgment until the first of September next.

| | |
|---|---|
| Phebe Martin | Plaintiff |
| vs | In Trespass |
| John Wells | Defendant |

On motion of the Defendant by his Counsel to grant praying an an appeal from the Judgment and Opinion of the Court to the next Superior Court of Law to be holden for the district of Adams which is granted upon his having entered into and acknowledged Bonds with Securities according to Law.

110

Accounts Audited

| | | |
|---|---|---|
| Henry Turner's a/c | 6 | 93-3/4 |
| Isaac Lauck | 9 | " |
| Anthony Daugherty of | 21 | 6¼ |
| Martin McWilliams | 20 | " |
| Doct<sup>r</sup> David Latimore | 65 | " |
| | 122 | 00 |

Thomas Grinnell Esquire having produced a Licence from his Excellency William C. C. Claiborne to practice as an attorney and counselor at law he having taken the usual oath is admitted accordingly.

Isaac Laucks having produced an account to the Court for Repairs done to the Jail which being examined is admitted and ordered to be Certified . . . 34 - 26'.

Ordered that Joseph Sessions be commissioned and William Loaman Surveyor on the part of this County to make Dividing line between same and Jefferson County and Wilkinson County to meet the persons appointed by Jefferson County at the House of Mr. George Sulcer in Ellicotteville on the fourth Monday in July next in order to proceed on Said Business and to meet the Commissioners appointed by Wilkinson County at the House of Mr. Nathan Swayze in the Jury Settlement on the Second Monday in September next for the Same purpose and that the Clerk make out Copies of this Order and enclose to each of the Clerks of Said Court and also the Commissioners & Surveyors on the part of this County.

---

111

Justices appointed by the Court to take & Receive lists of the taxable property in the County:

| Justices | | District |
|---|---|---|
| James Neillson | given | Abner L. Duncan |
| William Darby | do | William Darby |
| John Irwin | given | Benj. Holmes |
| John Callender | do | Wades |
| Joseph Sessions | given | Sessions |
| Abner Green | given | Jesse Carter |
| A. Montgomery | do | David Greenlief |
| Jacob Guice | given | Guice |
| F. L. Claiborne | do | William Nichols |
| Caleb King | | James Hoggatt |
| | | Israel Luse |
| | | Philander Smith |

Court Adjourned until Monday Morning nine o'clock.

Monday 13$^{th}$ June The Court according to Adjournment met
Present
Sam$^l$ Brooks
James Ferrell
James Matson     Esquires
&
Abner Green

The commissioners appointed to view the most Convenient way for Roads in Captain Duncan's District this day returned their Report, to wit, "From the St Catharine's Bridge to the Town of Washington following the Road laid out and marked by the Commissioners heretofore in pursuance of an act of assembly entitled an act

Authorizing the making a way for a public Road from the Boundary line near Pineridgeville to the Grind Stone ford on the Bayou pierre from thence along to old Road as it now runs to the muddy fork of St Catharine being the Boundary of the aforesaid militia District also one other road from the Bridge called King's Bridge on the St Catharine Creek along the old way as now and to Abram Taylor's plantation, the fence of Christian Harmon to be removed inwards so to give Sufficient Space to the road, also one other Road leading from the plantaion of Adam Tooley to the town of Washington along the way now used except only along the fence of David Gibson's Field the Road to run as the Said fence leads, the Same Said Gibson having already Suited the course of his fence to that of the road as laid out by us, also one other Road leading from Christian Harmon's plantation to the town of Washington opened agreeable to the Course marked and laid out by David Burney whereupon it is ordered that the same be recorded.

Ezekiel Headies Act
Being produced in Court for his Services in Assisting to lay off prison Bounds was Examined and allowed -    2
Thomas Hanes Act                                                28.42
The following Gentlemen appointed to receive Taxable property in the District which they belong

   District
   Capt$^n$ Smith      Charles Surget
   Capt Hoggatt Given Howard Adam Tooley

Leonard Pomet     Plaintiff
 vs         In Case
James McNeely     Defendant

This day came the parties by their attorneys and Thereupon came also a Jury to wit Sam$^l$ Moore, Washington Stubblefield, Andrew Abrams, John Cammack, William Clarke, John Martin, John Irwin, John Calliham and Thomas Ford, John Foster, Ezekiel Dowitt & William Cochran who being elected tried and Sworn well and truly to try the issue Joined upon their oath do Say that the Defendant ~~is~~ did ~~guilty~~ assume in manner and form as the plaintiff in his Declaration against him hath declared and do assess the plaintiff Damages by occasion thereof to two hundred and fifty five Dollars also his Costs by him about his Suit in this behalf expended and the Said Defendant in Mercy &c.         Sam$^l$ P. Moore, foreman.

 John Bustrick     Plaintiff
  Vs         in Case
 Ebenezer Rees     Defendant

This day came the plaintiff by his attorney and the Defendant in proper person and the Said Defendant acknowledges the plaintiff's action, therefore it is Considered by the Court that the plaintiff recover against the Said Defendant the sum one hundred and Eighty nine Dollars and ninety nine Cents also his Costs by him about his suit in this behalf expended and the Said Defendant in Mercy &c and the plaintiff agrees to Stay the Ex$^{or}$ of this Judgment till the first of September next.

| | |
|---|---|
| John Rapllee | Plaintiff |
| Vs | In Case |
| Patrick Connelly et al | Defendant |

This day came the plaintiff by his attorney and the Defendant in proper person and the Said Defendant acknowledges the plaintiff's action therefore it is considered by the Court that the plaintiff recover against the Said Deft the sum of one hundred and twenty eight Dollars and eleven and one half cent also his Costs by him about his Suit in this behalf expended and the said Defendant in Mercy &c agree to Stay Ex$^{or}$ of this Judgment till first of September next.

| | |
|---|---|
| Woisger | Plaintiff |
| vs | |
| Strickland | Defendant |

Plea of non trial Record replication and Joinder

| | |
|---|---|
| William Loan | Plaintiff |
| vs | In Trover |
| Patrick Connally | Defendant |

Mr. Abijah Hunt comes into Court and as ad$^{tor}$ of Philip Noname Declared and agrees to Deliver up the notes given by Loan for the Horses in the Declaration mentioned and to pay the Costs of this Suit.

Ordered that Col$^{l}$ John Girault, Benjamine Kitchens & Jeremiah Ruth, Gen., view and mark out such roads as may be necessary to be opened in the District formally Captain Wades' and make report thereof to the next Court

---

| | |
|---|---|
| Stewart | Plaintiff |
| Vs | in /Blank/ |
| Truly | Defendant    Rule of Reference |

The parties agree to Refer all matters in Difference to the Declaration of Ebenezer Rees and James Neilson Esquires whose award to be returned into the Clerk's office in two months and Execution to Issue thereon.

| | |
|---|---|
| David Ferguson & Woolley | Plaintiff |
| Versus | in Case |
| John King | Defendant |

This day came the parties by their attornies and thereof came also a Jury to wit Peter A. Vandorn, Washington Stubberfield, Andrew Abrams, John Cammick, William Clarke John Martin, John Irwin, John Callaham, Thomas Ford, John Foster, Moses Moore & William Cochran who being elected Tried and Sworn well and truly to enquire of Damages upon their oath do Say that the Defendant is guilty did assume in manner and form as the plaintiff in his Declaration ag$^{st}$ him hath Declared and do assess the plaintiff Damages by occasion thereof to three hundred and fifty Seven Dollars and seventy eight Cents and Costs of Suit therefore it is Considered by the Court that the plaintiff recover against the Said Defendant his Damages aforesaid in Manner and form by the Jurors in their virdict aforesaid assessed and also his Costs by him about his Suit this behalf expended and the Said Defendant in Mercy &c

|                | Mathew McCullock | Plaintiff |
|---|---|---|
| Recorded       | Vs               | In Case   |
| by P. Walker   | John O'Conner    | Defendant |

This day came the parties by their attornies and thereupon came also a Jury
to wit: Peter Vandorn, Washington Stubbefield, Andrew Adams, John Cammick,
William Clarke, John Martin, John Irwin, John Calliham, Thomas Ford, John
Foster, Moses Moore & William Cochran who being elected tried and Sworn well
and truly to enquire of Damages upon their oath do say that the Defendant is
Guilty in Manner and form as the as the plaintiff ag$^{st}$ him hath declared and
65.99    do assess the plaintiff Damages by occasion to Sixty five Dollars
cor 5.38    ninety four cents and cost of Suit therefore it is Considered by the
$71.32    Court that the plaintiff recover against the Said Defendant his Dam-
ages aforesaid assessed and also his costs by him about his suit in
this behalf expended and the Said Defendant in Mercy &c.

|             | John Prior Perkins | Plaintiff |
|---|---|---|
| Recorded    | vs                 | in Debt   |
|             | George Cochran     | Defendant |

This day came the parties by their attornies and their upon came also a
Jury, to wit Peter Vandorn, Washington Stubblefield, Andrew Abrams, John
Calliham, Thomas Ford, John Foster, Moses Moore & William Cochran who being
elected tried and Sworn well & truly to enquire of damages upon their oaths,
do say that the Defendant is Guilty in Manner and form as the plaintiff in
his declaration ag$^{st}$ him hath complained and do assess the plaintiff Damages
by occasion thereof to

two hundred and Sixteen Dollars and Seventeen cents and Costs, therefore
it is Considered by the Court that the plaintiff recover against the Said
Defendant his Damages aforesaid in Manner and form by the Jurors in their
verdict aforesaid assessed and also his costs by him about his suit in this
behalf expended and the Said Defendant in Mercy &c

|             | David Ferguson & Woolley | Plaintiff |
|---|---|---|
| Recorded    | Vs                       | in Case   |
|             | William Atchinson        | Defendant |

This day came the parties by their attornies and thereupon came also a Jury
to wit Peter Vandorn, Washington Stubblefield, Andrew Abrams, John Cammick
William Clarke, John Martin, John Irwin, John Calliham, Thomas Ford, John
Foster, Moses Moore & William Cochran who being elected tried and Sworn
well and truly to enquire of Damages upon their oath do say that the Defendant is Guilty in manner and form as the plaintiff in their Declaration against him hath declared and do assess the plaintiff Damages by occasion thereof
to fifty one Dollars Seventy two and one half cents and Costs of Suit therefore it is considered by the Court that the plaintiff recover against the
Said Defendant his Damages aforesaid in Manner & form by the Jurors in their
Verdict aforesaid assessed and also his costs by him about his Suit in this
behalf expended and the Said Defendant in Mercy &c

|  |  |  |
|---|---|---|
| | Ext^or of Alex^r Moore | Plaintiff |
| Recorded | vs | in Case |
| | Henry Holston | Defendant |

This day came the plaintiff by his attorne and thereupon came also a Jury to wit Peter Vandorn, Washington Stubblefield, Andrew Abrams, John Cammick, William Clarke, John Martin, John Irwin, John Calligam, Thomas Ford, John Foster, Moses Moore, & William Cochran, who being elected tried and Sworn well and truly to enquire of Damages upon their oath do say that the Defendant ~~is guilty~~ did assume in manner and form as the plaintiff in his Declaration against him hath Declared and do assess the plaintiff's Damages by occasion thereof to three hundred and twenty three Dollars eighteen & one half cents and Costs of Suit therefore it is Considered by the Court that the plaintiff recover against the Said Defendant his Damages aforesaid in manner and form by the Jurors in their verdict aforesaid assess^d and also his Costs by him about his Suit in this behalf expended and the Said Defendant in Mercy &^c

|  |  |  |
|---|---|---|
| | Ex^tors M. Stackpoole | Plaintiff |
| | vs | In Case |
| | Thomas Dorrock | Deft |

This day came the parties by their Attornies and thereupon came also a Jury to wit, Peter Vandorn, Washington Stubblefield, Andrew Abrams, John Cammick, William Clarke, John Irwin, John Calliham, Thomas Ford, John Foster, Moses Moore & William Cochran, who being elected tried and Sworn well and truly to enquire of Damages upon their oath do say that the Defendant is Guilty in Manner & form as the plaintiff in his Declaration against him hath alledged and and do assess the plaintiff damages

---

by occasion of his not performing the Several promises and undertakes aforesaid and Costs of suit therefore it is Considered by the Court that the plaintiff recover his Damages aforesaid in Manner and form by the Jurors in their verdict aforesaid assessed and also their costs by him about their Suit in this behalf expended and the Said Defendant in Mercy &^c

|  |  |  |
|---|---|---|
| | Morris Stackpoole | Plaintiff |
| Recorded | vs | In Case |
| | Henry Phipps | Defendant |

This day came the parties by their attornies and Thereupon came also a Jury to wit Peter Vandorn, Washington Stubblefield, Andrew Abrams, John Cammick, William Clarke, John Martin, John Irwin, John Callihan, Thomas Ford, John Foster, Moses Moore & William Cochran who being elected tried and Sworn well & truly to enquire of Damages in this suit upon their oaths do say that the plaintiff hath Sustained Damages by reason of the Defendant not performing this promise and undertaking in the Declaration ment^d to Sixty four Dollars and fifty seven cents besides his Costs of Suit therefore it is Considered by the Court that the plaintiff, recover against the Said Deft^t his Dang^s aforesaid in Manner and form by the Jurors in their verdict aforesaid assessed and also his Costs by him about his suit in this behalf expended and the Said Deft in Mercy &^c

|  |  |  |
|---|---|---|
| Recorded | John P. Perkins<br>vs<br>Gab Swayze & Is[1] Luce | Plaintiff<br>In Case<br>Defendant |

This day came the parties by their attornies and thereupon came also a Jury to wit Benjamin Kitchens, Washington Stubblefield, Andrew Abrams, John Cammick, William Clarke, John Martin, John Irwin, John Callihan, Thomas Ford, John Foster, William Cochran, & Moses Moore, who being elected tried and Sworn well and truly to enquire of Damages in this Suit upon their oath do say that the plaintiff hath Sustained Damages by reason of the Defendants nonperformance of this promise and undertaking in the Declaration mentioned to twenty Six Dollars and eighty Cents besides his costs of Suit therefore it is Considered by the Court that the plaintiff recover against the Said Defendant his Damages aforesaid in manner and form by the Jurors in their verdict aforesaid assessed and also his Costs by him about his Suit in this behalf expended and the Said Defendant in Mercy &c

|  |  |  |
|---|---|---|
| Recorded | Abijah Hunt<br>Vs<br>John Baptist Labrathre | Plaintiff<br>In Case<br>Defendant |

This day came the parties by their attornies and thereupon came also a Jury to wit, Benjamin Kitchez, Washington Stubblefield, Andrew Abrams John Cammick, William Clarke, John Martin, John Irwin, John Callihan, Thomas Ford, John Foster, William Cochran & Moses Moore who being elected tried and Sworn well and truly to enquire of Damages in this Suit upon the oath do Say that the plaintiff hath Sustained Damages by reason of the Defendant's nonperformance of his promise & undertaking in the Declaration Mentioned to one cent besides his Costs of Suit.

Therefore it is Considered by the Court that the plaintiff recover against the Said Defendant his Dam. aforesaid in Manner and form by the Jurors in their verdict aforesaid assess and also his Costs by him about his Suit in this behalf Expended and the Said Defendant in Mercy &c

|  |  |  |
|---|---|---|
| Recorded | Arthur Carney<br>vs<br>Ford Bryan and John Ferguson | Plaintiff<br>in Case<br>Defen[d] |

This day came the parties by their attornies and thereupon came also a Jury to Wit Benjamine Kitchens, Washington Stubblefield, Andrew Abrams, John Cammick, William Clarke, John Martin, John Irwin, John Callihan, Thomas Ford, John Foster, William Cochran & Moses Moore who being elected tried and Sworn well and truly to enquire of Damages upon their oath do Say that the plaintiff hath Sustained Damages by reason of the Defendants nonperformance of his promise and undertaking in the Declaration mentioned to Sixty Dollars and Costs of Suit Therefore it is considered by the Court that the plaintiff recover against the Said Defendant his Damages aforesaid in Manner and form by the Jurors in their verdict aforesaid assessed and also his costs by him about his Suit in this behalf expended and the Said Defendant in Mercy &c

|  | Thomas Regan | Plaintiff |
|---|---|---|
| Recorded | vs | In Case |
|  | Andrew Robinson | Defendant |

This day came the parties by their attornies and thereupon came also a Jury to Wit Benjamine Kitchens, Washington Stubblefield, Andrew Abrams, John Cammick, William Clarke, John Martin, John Irwin, John Calliham, Thomas Ford John Foster, William Cockran & Moses Moore who being elected tried and Sworn well & truly to enquire of Damages upon their oath do say that the plaintiff hath Sustained Damages by reason of the Def$^{ts}$ non performance of his promises and undertaking in the Declaration mentioned to fifty four dollars and Twenty five Cents and Costs of Suit Therefore it is Considered by the Court that the Plaintiff recover against the Said Defendant his Damages aforesaid in Manner and form by the Jurors in their verdict aforesaid assessed and also his Costs by him about his Suit in this behalf expended and the Said Defendant in Mercy &$^c$

|  | The Same | Plaintiff |
|---|---|---|
| Recorded |  | In Case |
|  | The Same | Defendant |

This day came the parties by their attornies and thereupon came also a Jury to wit, Benjamine Kitchens, Washington Stubblefield, Andrew Abrams, John Cammick, William Clarke, John Martin, John Irwin, John Calliham, Thomas Ford, John Foster, William Cochran & Moses Moore, who being elected tried and Sworn well and Truly to enquire of Damages in this Suit upon their oath do Say that the plaintiff hath Sustained Damages by reason of the Defendants non performance of his promise and undertaking in the Declaration Mentioned to one hundred and four Dollars and fifty Cents and Costs of Suit therefore it is considered by the Court that the plaintiff recover against the Said Defendant his Damages aforesaid in Manner and form by the Jurors in their Verdict aforesaid assessed and also his Costs by him about his Suit in this behalf expended and the Said Defendant in Mercy &$^c$

|  | Henry Barr | Plaintiff |
|---|---|---|
| Recorded | Vs | In Case |
|  | Jno Knilton | Defendant |

This day came the Parties by their Attornies and thereupon came also a Jury to wit, Benjamine Kitchens, Washington Stubblefield, Andrew Abrams, John Cammick, William Clarke, John Martin, John Irwin, John Calliham, Thomas Ford, John Foster, William Cochran & Moses Moore who being elected tried and Sworn well and truly to enquire of Damages upon their oath do Say that the plaintiff hath Sustained Damages by reason of the Defendants nonperformance of his promise and undertaking in the Declaration mentioned to forty two Dollars and forty eight Cents and costs of Suit, therefore it is Considered by the Court that the plaintiff recover against the Said Defendant his Damages aforesaid in Manner and form by the Jurors in their verdict aforesaid assessed and also his Costs by him about his Suit in this behalf expended and the Said Defendant in Mercy &$^c$

|  | William Barrow | Plaintiff |
|---|---|---|
| Recorded | vs | in Debt |
|  | Lake Whiting | Defendant |

This day came the plaintiff by his Attorney and The Defendant in proper person & the Said Defendant acknowledges the plaintiff's action Therefore it is Considered by the Court that the Plt Recover against the said Defendant the Sum of one hundred and Sixty one Dollars and also his Costs by him about his suit in this behalf expended and the Said Defendant in Mercy &c

|  | Samuel Timberlake & Hancock | Plaintiffs |  |
|---|---|---|---|
| Recorded | vs | in Debt |  |
|  | Barton Hannon | Deft | _____'s Death Suggested |

This day came the plaintiff by his attorney and the Defendant in proper person & the Said Defendant acknowledges the plaintiff's action Therefore it is considered by the Court that the plaintiff recover against the Said Defendant the Sum of Sixty nine Dollars and twenty five cents the Debt in the Declaration Mentioned also Six Dollars and Ninety nine Cents Damages and his Costs by him about his Suit in this behalf expended and the Said Defendant in Mercy &c and agree to stay exe$^n$ till first Sept.

|  | Thomas Wilkins | Plaintiff |
|---|---|---|
| Recorded | vs | in Case |
|  | Hardress Ellis | Defendant |

This day came the plaintiff by his attorney and the Defendant in proper person and the Said Defendant acknowledges the plaintiff's action therefore it is Considered by the Court that the plaintiff Recover against the said Defendant the Sum of Six Dollars & Eighty five cents and also his Costs by him about his Suit in this behalf expended and the Said Deft in Mercy &c & agree to the Ex$^{on}$ of this Judg$^t$ till first of Sept.

|  | William Dunbar | Plaintiff |
|---|---|---|
|  | vs | In Case |
|  | William B. Smith | Defendant |

This day came the plaintiff by his attorney and the Defendant in proper person and the Said Defendant acknowledges the plaintiff's action therefore it is Considered by the Court that the plaintiff recover against the Said Defendant the Sum of one hundred and twelve Dollars eighty seven and one half cents and also his Costs by him about his Suit in this behalf expended and the Said Defendant in Mercy &c and agree to Stay the execution of this Judgment till the first of September next.

|  | James Beauvias | Plaintiff |
|---|---|---|
| Recorded | Vs | in Debt |
|  | Reubin Gillick | Defendant |

This day came the plaintiff by his attorney and the Def in proper person and the Said Defendant acknowledges the plaintiff's action therefore it is Considered by the Court that the plaintiff recover against the Said Defendant the Sum of Sixty one Dollars eighty and one & half cents and also his Costs about his Suit in this behalf expended and the Said Defendant in Mercy &c with Stay of execution of this Judgment until first of September next.

|  |  |  |
|---|---|---|
| | Evans | Plaintiff |
| Recorded | vs | |
| | Reese | Defendant |

This day came the parties by their Attorneys and agree the pleadings in this Cause be made up before the next Court and the ~~Cause~~ Same is, is continued.

---

|  |  |
|---|---|
| Samuel Neilson | Plaintiff |
| Vs | In Debt |
| Lake Whiting | Defendant |

This day came the plaintiff by his Attorney and the Def$^t$ in proper person and the Said Defendant acknowledges the plaintiff's action therefore it is Considered by the Court that the plaintiff recover against the Said Def$^t$ the Sum of one hundred and two Dollars and eighteen Cents and three fourths Cents and also his Costs by him about his suit in this behalf expended and the Said Defendant in Mercy &$^c$ with Stay of execution of this Judgment three months.

|  |  |
|---|---|
| Wells | Plt |
| Vs | |
| Holland | Def$^t$ |

On Motion it is ordered that Mr. William Brookes appear on Wednesday next and Show Cause if any he can why an attachment Should not issue against him late Sheriff of the County for not bringing into Court two hundred and Twenty Seven Dollars and thirty five Cents Costs, Money Made on a venditions expense in the Case.

Deed from Juan Vidal & ux to Charles Forgett was acknowledged & togeather with Certificate of relinquishment of Dower thereon endorsed and ordered to be recorded.

---

|  |  |
|---|---|
| Isaac Guion | Plaintiff |
| vs | in Case |
| Benjamine Kitchens | Defendant |

This day came the plaintiff by his attorney and the Defendant in proper person and the Said Defendant acknowledges the plaintiff's action. Therefore it is Considered by the Court that the plaintiff recover against the Said Defendant fifty Dollars and also his Costs by him about his Suit in this behalf expended and the Said Def$^t$ in Mercy &$^c$ with stay of ex$^{on}$ of the Judg$^{dt}$ two Months.

|  |  |
|---|---|
| McWilliams | Plaintiff |
| vs | In /Blank/ |
| Kitchens | Defendant |

The parties in this Suit agree to submit all Matters in Difference between them to the final Determination of Arthur Andrews & William T. McCormick whose award to be returned into the Clerk's office in two Months and Execution to Issue against the party against Whom the Balance Shall be found.

Court adjourned until tomorrow Morning 9 o'clock.

Court Met according to adjournment
Present
Samuel Brooke
Abner Green
&
James Neilson
Esquires

Recorded

Seth Caston
   vs
Lewis Evans

Plaintiff
In Case
Defendant

This day came the parties by their attornies and the the Said Defendant relinquishing his former plea acknowledges the plaintiff's action. Therefore it is Considered by the Court that the plaintiff recover ag$^{st}$ the said Defendant the sum of one hundred and twenty eight Dollars and twenty one Cents and also his Costs by him about his Suit in this behalf expended and the Said Defendant in Mercy &$^c$ with Stay of Ex$^{on}$ of this Judgment until Next Term.

Absent Sam$^l$ Brookes
Present Wm Darby

Thomas Rogan
   vs
Benjamin Kitchens

Plaintiff
in /Blank/
Defendant     Rule Reference

The parties in this Suit agree to submit all Matters in Difference between them to the final determination of Ferdinand L. Clairborn and John Henderson Esquire whose award to be returned into the Clerk's office in two Months and execution to issue thereon.

George Poindexter having produced a Licence from his Excellency William C. Claiborne to practice as an attorney and Counsellor at Law whereupon he took the usual oaths & is admitted accordingly.

James Moore
   vs
Richard Miller

Plaintiff
In Case
Defendant

The parties in the Suit Waved the trial of the Issue by a Jury and agree to put themselves on the Judg$^{nt}$ of the Court and being heard it is the opinion of the Court that the Damages be released and that the Plt. recover against the Defendant his Costs by him about his Suit in this behalf expended and the Said Defendant in Mercy &$^c$.

Same
   Vs
John King

Plaintiff
in Case
Def$^t$

This day came the parties by their attornies and waved the trial of the Issue by a Jury and agree to put themselves on the Judgment of the Court & being fully heard it is the opinion of the Said Defendant be released of the Damages and that the plaintiff recover against the Defendant his Costs by him about his Suit in this behalf expended and the Said Defendant in Mercy &$^c$

                Douglass                    Plaintiff
                   vs                       In /Blank/
                Green                       Deft
This day came the parties by their attornies and Therefore came also a Jury
to wit, Nathaniel Tomlinson, Samuel Moore, Charles McBride, Niel McCann,
John Foster, Abram Gaultney, William Cochran, John Irwin, John Martin, Thomas
Ford, Ezekiel Dewitt, & William Clarke, Sam¹ Moore one of the Jurors with-
drawn by Consent & pleadings to be made up and continued.

---

                              130

                Fitzgerald                  Plaintiff
                   vs                       in /Blank/
                Kitchens                    Deft            Rule Reference
The parties came into Court and agree to Submit all Matters if Difference to
Love Baker the plaintiff to Give the Defendant five day notice of the time
and place on or before the first day of September next or Suit to be Dismiss-
ed 10ᵗʰ September Dismissed.
    William Books account of one hundred and twenty Six Dollars and Eighty
Seven and one half Cents was is allowed and ordered to be Certified.
                                    Absent Williams Darby Esqr.
                                    Present John Callender Esqr.
    A. Hutchins produced in Court an account of his mark and Brand used in
Designating his live Stock which is ordered to be recorded.
    John Hutchins produced in open Court an acc^t of his mark and Brand used
in Designating his live Stock which is ordered to be recorded.
    Ordered that the report of the Pine Ridge Road be laid over until next.
    Ordered that all the Causes of the United States to which any appear-
ances have been entered, be continued until the next Court.
    Court adjourned until tomorrow morning 9 o'clock.

---

                              131

                            Court Met according to adjournment 15th
                                    Present
                                    Sam¹ Brookes     Esquires
                                    John Henderson
                                        &
                                    William Darby
    Sam¹ Brookes Esquire produced an Act in Court which being examined is
allowed and ordered to be Certified.                    $6
        James Noilson              Ditto               15
        ditto   do                  do                 14
          do    do                  Do                 12 50
        ditto   do                  Do                  5
          do    do                  do                  8
          do    do                  do                  9
          do    do                  do                 24 75     73.25
        William Nicholls            do                 13-90
        John Henderson              do                  4
        Same as overseer of the poor                   13 50
                                                      125 65

Abner Duncan          Plaintiff
vs                   Attach$^t$
Craig                 Defendant

Henry Turner as Garnishee being Sworn declares that he has in his hands One hundred dollars belonging to the Defendant & Stay of proceedings Six months and the Clerk is Ordered to forward a notification for the Defendant to appear and plead.

---

132

Farrar                Plaintiff
vs                   in /Blank/
Rees                 Defendant

On Motion it is ordered that the order of Reference in this Suit be set aside.

Seth Lewis Esquire Records his Stock mark and Brand as follows to wit: A crop and a slit in the right Ear an under bit in the left ear and his brand S. L.

On the motion of Samuel Hutchins by his Counsel to quash the Report appointed to view and mark out the most convenient way for Roads in what is called Captain Carter's Districts Relative to that Road within Said Districts which runs thr° the Said Samuel Hutchins Lands which motion was objected to by the Counsel in the oposite Side alledging that the Court have no Jurisdiction, thereupon it is the opinion of the Court that they have jurisdiction & Controul over the proceedings of the Said Jury it is ordered that the said report be quashed for irregularity appearing on the face of the proceedings and that they will take no Further Notice of Said Report.

Court adjourned till 9 O'clock the following Day Thursday 16$^{th}$.

                       Court met according to adjournment
                                   Present
                                   John Henderson
                                   Abner Green        Esquires
                                   William Darby

---

133

An Indenture of Bargain and Sale from David Gibson & Uxor to James A. Mathews was acknowledged by the Said David & together with the Certificate of the relinquishment of Dower and ordered to be recorded.

James Wallace produced his account in Court for laying off prison bounds and Surveying, was examined and ordered to be certified.      $29

Robert Stanfield        Plaintiff
Vs                       Atta
George Lawin            Defendant

This day came the parties by their attorneys and thereupon the Defendants plea in Abatement in this Cause being Argued it is the opinion of the Court that the law is for the Defendant, Therefore it is Considered by the Court that the plaintiffs Suit be Dismissed and the Defendant go hence without Day and recover against the plaintiff his Costs by him about him in this behalf expended.

|  |  |
|---|---|
| Pomet | Plaintiff |
| Vs | in /Blank/ |
| McNeelly | Defendant |

The Defendant in this cause by his attorney comes and prays an appeal to the next Superior Court of law; he having entered into & acknowledged bond in the Sum of Six hundred Dollars with James Wallace & David Johnston his Securities conditioned as the Law requires and is granted.

Charles McBride presented an account of fifty nine Dollars and eight cents which being ex$^{od}$ is allowed and ordered to be certified.

The Account of the Clerk for Stationary is Ordered to be continued for Consideration

Absent
John Henderson
Abner Green   Esquires

Present
Sam$^l$ Brooks
John Callender   Esquires

Ezekiel Heady Acc$^t$ Audited and ordered to be certified
for: $8.

| Certified | John Smith | 3. |
|---|---|---|
| Certified | Robert Baskford | 52.40 |
| Certified | John Holley | 433.40 |
|  |  | 526.80 |

|  |  |
|---|---|
| Moore | Plaintiff |
| vs | In /Blank/ |
| Strikland | Defendant |

John Holley comes into Court and undertakes for the Deft That in case he be cast in this Suit that he will Satisfy and pay the Costs and condemnation of the Court Surrender his body in execution to prison for the Same or in Case of failure thereof the the Said Holly will do it for him.

|  |  |
|---|---|
| Perkins | Plaintiff |
| Vs |  |
| Cochran | Defendant |

The parties in the above Suit by Consent pray an Appeal to the Superior Court without lay on either part.

|  |  |
|---|---|
| Benjamine Stokes | Plaintiff |
| V |  |
| Winthrop Sargent | Defendant |

The Defendant in this Cause by his counsel pray an appeal from the Judgment of this Court to the next

Superior Court of Law he having entered into and acknowledged Bond with Lyman Harding and his Securities in the Sum of two hundred Dollars Conditioned according to Law.

Court adjourned till Court in Course.

Daniel Grafton presented an account of his live Stock used in Designating them to wit: a crop on the left ear and on the right ear half crop. Brand D.G. on the left Buttock

Signed<br>D. Grafton

At a Court held for the County of Adams at the court house thereof in the City of Natchez on Monday the third day of October in the year of our Lord one thousand eight hundred and three & in the 28th year of American Independance.

Present:
Samuel Brooks
Joseph Seselers    Esquires
James Ferrall
William Foster

Andrew Marschalk Esq Produced an account in Court for Building Stocks and Pillory & Whiping posts amounting to ninety two Dollars and forty one and one fourth cent which being examined by the Court was allowed that is to Say one half of said sum be paid out of the County treasury the City of Natchez having agreed to pay the other half thereof which is ordered to be certified accordingly.

| | | |
|---|---|---|
| Wal atto John Reed | Plaintiff | |
| Wd For      vs | In Case | |
| Costs   John Perkins | Defendant | |
| 5.50 | | |

This day came the Plafft by his Attornies and the Defendant in Person & Relinquishing his former plea Acknowledges the plaintiff's action therefore it is Considered by the Court that the plaintiff recover against the said Defendant the sum of thirty Dollars with lawful Interest from the tenth day of February 1803 till paid desides his Costs by him about his Suit in this behalf expended and the Said defendant in Mercy &c and the plaintiff agrees to Stay execution of this Judg$^t$ Six weeks.

On the petition Charles King ordered that a Licence be Granted him to keep a tavern at his house in this County for and during the term of one year from the date hereof and and until the next Succeeding County Court thereafter whereupon the Said Charles with John Cammick and John Boles his Sureties entered into and acknowledged Bond in the Sum of three hundred dollars Conditioned according to Law.

Absalom Griffin who was fined at the last term for having made default as a Juror this day filed an Affidavit of his inability to attend at Said Term in these words to wit; "Personally appeared before me John Henderson one of the Justices of the Peace for Said County and made oath the reason he did not attend as a Juryman at the June Court held for the Said County of Adams was his having cut his leg with an ax in Such a manner that he was Disabled to attend the Said Court. Given under my hand this 3$^{rd}$ Oct. 1803 sworn before me John Henderson, J. P." whereupon his fine is remitted.

Ordered the Court to adjd till tomorrow 10 O'clock.

Court according to adjournment met Tuesday Oct 4$^{th}$ 1803
Present
Samuel Brooks
Joseph Sessions    Esquires
and F. L. Claiborne

Samuel May who made oath in open court that Peter Walker Jun$^r$ of the City of Natchez was the Author of a Contempt offered to the dignity of this Court it is ordered that an attachment do Issue against the Said Peter returnable amediatly commanding the Sheriff to bring the body of the Said Peter before the Court to do and receive what in this behalf shall be adjudged and the Sheriff of the County Ret$^d$ that he taken the body of the Offender

138

Whereupon the Said Peter Walker, Jun$^r$, Lewis Evans and John Garrett, Personally appeared in Court and acknowledged themselves to be severally indebted to his Excellency William C. C. Claiborne Governor of the Mississippi Territory the Said Peter in the Sum of three hundred Dollars and the Said Lewis Evans and John Garrett in the sum of one hundred dollars, each to be levied of their respective Goods & chattles, Lands and Tenements with this condition that the Said Peter Walker shall make his personal appearance before this Court on Thursday the fourth Day of the present term and Shall not depart thence without leave of the Said Court then this Recognizance to be void otherwise to be in full force & virtue and now at this day to wit on Thursday the fourth day of this Said term.

Present
Samuel Brooks
Ferdinand L. Claiborne
James Neilson
Jonathan Guice         Esq$^{rs}$
Joseph Irwin
John Henderson
Wm Darby
&
James Farrall

Peter Walker Jun$^r$ who Stands bound by his Recognizance appeared in discharge thereof and the Said Peter having acknowledged to the Satisfaction of the Court that he the Said Peter had no intention to Injure

Ordered by the Court that County Certificates be taken for Taverns License in Said County which to be used in the County Treasurer.

the Judiciary nor was the Contempt offered to the dignity of this Court
with any intention to hurt or injure the feelings of any one of its Members and that he Drew a figure on the Wall without thought or intention
as expressed which acknowledgement being thought sufficient and received
by the Court the Said Peter is discharged.

---

### 139

David Ker former Clerk of this Court Exhibited an account against the
County for Stationary provided by an order of this Court which after Examination was allowed for thirty three Dollars and fifty Cents and ordered to
be Certified.

|  |  |
|---|---|
| James Farrell | Plaintiff |
| vs | In Debt |
| John Swayze | Defendant |

Charles King the Defendant's appearance Bail this Day Delivered up the body
of the Defendant in Discharge of this Recognizance Whereupon Gideon Hopkins
comes into Court and undertakes for the Defendant that in case he shall be
cast in this Suit he Shall Satisfy and pay the Costs and condemnation of the
Court or render his body to prison in Execution for the same or in case of
failure thereof that he Gideon Hopkins will do it for him.

|  |  |  |
|---|---|---|
|  | Ebenezer Rees | Plaintiff |
| Duncan | VS | In Case |
| Knox | Arthur Cobb | Defendant |

This day came the Plaintiff by his counsel and prayed that the Judgment
Obtained herein against him at the last Court may be Set aside whereupon
for Reasons offered to the the court a new Trial is Granted him.

|  |  |
|---|---|
| Ex^tor William Gilbert | Plff^t |
| vs | In Case |
| Job & R. Koris | Deft |

By Consent of the parties is ordered that this Suit be continued until Next
Court.

---

### 140

|  |  |
|---|---|
| John Willson | Plaintiff |
| vs | in /Blank/ |
| Ex^tors Monsantoes | Deft |

by Consent of the parties it is ordered that the Suit be continued till the
next Court.

|  |  |
|---|---|
| St James Beauveis & Co. | Plaintiff |
| VS | In Debt |
| Ex^tors Morris Stackpoole | Defendant |

by Consent of the parties it is ordered that this Suit be continued till the
next Court.

|  |  |
|---|---|
| John Crowe | Plt |
| vs | In Debt |
| John E. Long | Defendant |

This day came the Defendant by James Wallace his attorney and the Plaintiff the Solemnly called came not but made default nor is his Suit further Prosecuted, Therefore it is considered by the Court that the plaintiff be non Suited and that the Defendant go hence without Day and recover against the Plaintiff his Costs by him about his ~~suit~~ Defence in this behalf expended.

    David Ferguson               Plt
Drum.      vs
Mak.    David Harvard             Defendant

This day came the Parties by their attornies and agree to Submit all matters in Difference between them to David Gibson and Joseph Harrison to meet on the third Monday in this month at Mrs. Reeds in Washington at ten O'clock unto Meridian ~~and~~ to Report into the Clerk's office and execution to Issue thereon as Judgment of this term and all other notice waved.

---

                                141

Turner    Edward Plain            Plt
            vs                           In Case
        Garrott E. Pendergrast    Defendant

This day came the plaintiff by his attorney and the Defendant in Proper Person and the Said Defendant acknowledges the Plaintiff's action therefore it is Considered by the Court that the plaintiff recover against the Said Defendant the Sum of Seventy two dollars and seventy five Cents and Also his Costs by him about his Suit in this behalf and the Said Defendant in Mercy &c. and the plaintiff agrees to stay execution first Febry

        James Craig              Plaintiff
            vs                           in Case
        The Same                Defendant

This day came the plaintiff by his attorney and the Defendant in proper person and the Said Defendant acknowledges the Pltf's action Therefore it is considered by by the Court that the Plaintiff Recover against the Said Defendant the sum of two hundred and Sixty Dollars and also his Costs by him about his Suit in this behalf expended and the Said Defendant in Mercy &c with Stay till first Febry.

        George Rapalie           Plft
            vs                           In [Blank]
        John E. Long             Defend

By Consent of the Parties it is Ordered that the Suit be Continued until the next term.

---

                                142

        Thomas Green             Plt
            vs                           Atta
        Reed & Ford               Defendants

Order for taking the disposition of Parker Carradine Senr before David Phillips Esquire upon twenty four hours notice during the Setting of the County Court of Jefferson.

        Nataniel Tomlinson       Plaintiff
            vs                           Rule Reference
        Seth Caston               Defendant

The parties by their attornies Come into Court and Mutually Submit all matters in Difference between them in this cause to the final determination of Abner Green, Philander Smith, & Israel Smith or any two of the above named their their award to be returned into office in two Months from this date and execution to Issue thereon the Said Seth Caston to pay the cost of this Suit.

  Daniel Douglass      Plaintiff
    Vs           In Case
  Henry Green       Defendant

By consent of the parties it is ordered that this Suit be continued till the next Court.

  John Wilson        Plaintiff
    vs           In Case
  Lewis Evans       Defendant

Ordered that a Scire facias Issue to revive the Suit.

---

Wal   John King & R. Sackett    Plaintiff
Recorded    Vs           In Cov$^t$
Mah   Sam$^l$ Ashland & Joseph Strong   Def$^{ts}$

This day came the Plaintiff by his attorney and the Defendant in proper person and the Said Defendant acknowledges the plaintiff's action therefore it is Considered by the Court that the Plaintiff recover against the Said Defendant the sum of five Dollars and forty one Cents and also his Costs by him about his suit in this behalf expended and the Said Defendant in Mercy &c.

  Benjamine Goodwin     P$^{lt}$
    Vs          Trover & Con
Har   Robert Bashford      Defendant

This day came the Defendant by his Attorney and the Plaintiff tho Solemnly Called came not but made default nor is his Suit further Prosecuted therefore on the Prayer of the Def$^t$ it is Considered by the Court that the plaintiff be non Suited and the Defendant go hence without day and recover of of the Plaintiff his Costs by him about his Suit in this behalf expended.

  Garrett E. Pendergraft    Plaintiff
    vs          In Case
  Martin Henderlidor Ad$^{tor}$   Defendant

By Consent of the parties it is ordered that this suit by Dismissed at the Defendant's Costs.

  The Same        P$^{ltf}$
    vs          in Case
  The Same        Def$^t$

Dismissed at Defendants Costs.

| | | |
|---|---|---|
| Bra | Ebenezer Rees | Plaintiff |
| | vs | Case |
| | Lewis Duvill | Defendant |

This day came the plaintiff by his Attorney and the Said Defendant being Solemnly Called came not nor doth he say anything in bar or Preclusion of the Plaintiff's action whereby the Said Plaintiff thereof Remaineth against him altogether therein undefended therefore it is considered by the Court that the Plaintiff Recover against the Said Defendant his damages Sustained by occasion of the Defendants non performance of the Promise and undertaking in the Declaration mentioned and because it is not known what Damages the plaintiff hath Sustained, it is ordered that the Same assessed and enquired of by a Jury at the next Term.

| | | |
|---|---|---|
| Duncan | Simon and Benjamine Hook | Plaintiff |
| | vs | Trespass |
| Wal | Joseph Strong | Defendant |

Order by the Court that a Didimus Issue for taking the Disposition of Benjamine Ashlock before James Neilson Esquire at Washington on ten days notice to be given to the Adverse Party of the time of taking thereof.

Ordered that Court be adjourned till tomorrow Morning 9 O'clock.

---

145

Court according to adjournment met
Present
Sam'l Brooks Esq.

Ordered Court be adjourned till 3 O'clock.
three O'clock Court Agreeable to adjournment Met
Present
Samuel Brooks
John Henderson    Esqs.
&
Jonathan Guice

| | | |
|---|---|---|
| Har | Daniel Weisiger | Plaintiff |
| | Vs | In Debt |
| Mah | Joseph Strickland | Defendant |

This day came the parties by their Attornies and the Defts relinquishing his former plea acknowledges the Plaintiff's Action therefore it is Considered by the Court that the Plaintiff recover against the Said Defendant the Debt in the Declaration mentioned of one hundred and Sixteen Dollars and forty nine cents the debt in the Dec$^l$ mentioned also for his damages he hath sustained by reason of the detendion of S$^d$ Debt as for his thirty three Dollars and twenty five Cents his Costs by him about his Suit in this behalf expended and the Said Defendant in Mercy &c and the plaintiff agrees to Stay the execution of this Judgment till the first of Feb$^{ry}$.

(146-147)

146

|  |  |
|---|---|
| Daniel Douglass | Plaintiff |
| Recorded Vs | In Case |
| William McWilliams | Defendant |

This day came the parties by their Attornies and thereupon came a Jury to wit: Nathan Swayze, Gideon Hopkins, James West, John Boles John Armstreet, Archabald Evans, Ch$^s$ King, Christopher Harmon, Jesse Bell, John Calvit, Anthony Calvit, & Alexander Farrar who being elected tried and Sworn well and truly to try the Issue Joined upon their oath do Say that the ~~Plaintiff~~ Deft did assume upon himself in Manner and form as the plaintiff against him hath declared and do assess the Plaintiff damages by reason of that assumption to one hundred and thirty Dollars and thirty Seven and one half cents and his costs of suit.

Therefore it is considered by the Court that the Plaintiff recover against the Said Defendant his Damages aforesaid in Manner and form by the Jurors in their Verdict aforesaid assessed and also his Costs by him about his Suit in this behalf expended and the Said Defendant in Mercy &$^c$.

|  |  |
|---|---|
| Samuel Mull | Plaintiff |
| vs | in Case |
| David Johnston Adt$^{ors}$ | Defendant |

This day came the Defendant by his attorney prays & hath leave to impart till the first of Dec$^r$ next then to plead.

147

|  |  |
|---|---|
| Thomas Regan | Plaintiff |
| vs | in /Blank/ |
| Benjamine Kitchens | Defendant |

By consent of the parties it is ordered by the Court that the former Rule of Reference made herein at the last term be continued.

|  |  |
|---|---|
| Edmund L. Harris | Plaintiff |
| vs | in /Blank/ |
| Benjamine Kitchens | Defendant |

On the Motion of the plaintiff by his counsel it is ordered that this suit be Dismissed.

|  |  |  |
|---|---|---|
| Her | William Kenner | Plaintiff |
| Recorded | vs | in Case |
| Dun | Frederick Croner | Defendant |

This day came the parties by their attornies and the Deft relinquishing his former plea acknowledges the plaintiff's Action therefore it is Considered by the Court that the plaintiff recover against the Said Defendant the sum of fifty seven Dollars Subject however to any Declaration that the Defendant do make appear by the Report of Love Baker & James Wilkins provided that their award be returned into office in three months until which time the Execution is Stayed.

148

|  | Thomas Irwin | Plaintiff |
|---|---|---|
|  | v | in [Blank] |
|  | Charles Caston | Defendant |

By consent of the parties it is ordered that this suit be continued till the next court.

| Braz | Thomas Sullivan | Plaintiff |
|---|---|---|
|  | vs | in Case |
| V Cal | William Thompson | Defendant |

This day came the Defendant by his attorney and the Plaintiff, tho solemnly called, came not but made default nor is his suit further Prosecuted, therefore it is ordered by the Court that Plaintiff be non Suited and that the Defendant go hence without day and recover of the plaintiff his Costs by him about his Suit in this behalf expended.

| Bra |  The Same | Plaintiff |
|---|---|---|
|  | vs | in Case |
| Wal | Joseph Griffin | Deft |

Same order as next above

| Dun | Ebenezer Rees | Plaintiff |
|---|---|---|
|  | vs | in Case |
|  | Moses Carroll | Deft |

This day came the Parties by their attornies and the Defendant Relinquishing his former plea acknowledges the plaintiff's action therefore it is considered by the court that the Plaintiff recover the Said Defendant in the Sum of one hundred and eleven Dollars fifty Six and one fourth Cents which the parties here agree to be liquidated by the Clerk and also his Costs by him about his suit in this behalf expended and the Said Defendant in Mercy &c and the plaintiff agrees to stay the execution of this letter till the first of Feb$^{ry}$.

---

149

|  | John Fitzgerald | Plaintiff |
|---|---|---|
|  | vs |  |
|  | Benjamine Kitchens | Defendant |

The plaintiff failing to appear and Prosecute his suit it is ordered that the Same be dismissed.

| Dunlop | Joseph B. Ormsby | Plaintiff |
|---|---|---|
| Recorded | vs | in Case |
| Duncan | Ebenezer Rees | Defendant |

This day came the Parties by their attornies and thereupon came also a Jury to wit, Nathan Swayze, Gideon Hopkins, James West, John Boles, John Armstreet, Archibald Evans, Christian Harmon, Jessie Bell, Bennet Truly, Phillip Hoggatt, Stephen Douglass and Moses Moore who being elected tried and Sworn well and truly to try the Issue Joined whereupon by consent of the Parties and with the Assent of the Court Moses Moore one of the Jurors aforesaid was withdrawn and the rest of the Jurors from rendering their Verdict are Discharged and the Said Defendant relinquishing his former Plea acknowledges the Plaintiff's action for one hundred and fifty one Dollars and twenty five cents Damages and Costs of Suit, therefore it is Considered by the Court that the plaintiff recover against the Said Def$^t$ his Damages aforesaid and his costs by him about his suit in this behalf expended and the Said Defendant in Mercy &c and the Plaintiff agrees to Stay the Execution of Judg$^t$ till the first Day of April next.

| | | |
|---|---|---|
| Har | Joseph Singleton | Plaintiff |
| Recorded | Vs | in Case |
| Turner | George Hamilton | Defendant |

This day came the parties by their Attornies and thereupon came a Jury to wit, Nathan Swayze, Gideon Hopkins, James West, John Boles, John Armstreet, Archibald Evans, Christopher Harmon, Jesse Bell, Bennett Truly Philip Hoggatt, Stephen Douglass and Moses Moore who being elected tried and Sworn well and truly to try the Issue Joined upon their oath do Say that the Defendant did assume upon himself in Manner and form as the Plaintiff against him hath declared and do assess the Plaintiff Damages by reason of that assumption to forty Dollars besides Costs, Therefore it is considered by the court that the Plaintiff recover against the Said Defendant his Damages Aforesaid in Manner and form by the Jurors in their Verdict aforesaid assessed and also his costs by him about his suit in this behalf expended and the said Defendant in Mercy &$^c$

| | | |
|---|---|---|
| | David Ferguson & Melling Wooley | Pltff |
| | vs | In Case |
| | Andrew Beal | Def$^t$ |

The Defendant's Death being Suggested it is ordered by the Court that a Citation Issue against the Executors of the Said Deceased to come forward and Defend this Suit.

| | | |
|---|---|---|
| Wal | John Wells | Plts |
| | vs | Notice |
| | William Brooks late Sheriff | Def$^t$ |

The present Sheriff having returned that he had Served this notice on the former Sheriff for this County whereupon the plaintiff by his Counsel moved the Court for the Amt. of the Judgment the Said William returned to have made on a venditione Exponas at the Suit of the Said John Wells against John Holland and by consent of the Parties it is ordered that this Motion be continued till tomorrow.

Ordered that Court be adjourned till tomorrow morning 9 o'clock.

Thursday October 6$^{th}$ 1803 met agreeable to adjournment
Present
Samuel Brooks
Jonathan Guice

Ferdinand L. Claiborne

| | | |
|---|---|---|
| | St James Beauvies &c. | Pltff$^s$ |
| Recorded | Vs | in Case |
| | Patrick Connally | Def$^t$ |

This day came the Parties by their Attornies and Defendant relinquishing his former Plea acknowledges the plaintiff's action therefore it is considered by the Court that the Plaintiff recover against the Said Defendant the Sum of Seventy Dollars and ninety four cents and also his Costs by him about his Suit in this behalf expended and the Said Defendant in Mercy &$^c$

| | | |
|---|---|---|
| Dun | Patrick Kirkpatrick | Plaintiff |
| | vs | in /Blank/ |
| Hard | Ezra Johns | Defendant |

On the Motion of the Plaintiff by his counsel it is ordered that this suit be dismissed

| | |
|---|---|
| Thomas Johnston | Pltff |
| vs | |
| Peter Anthony | Deft |

This day came the Defendants by his attorney and the Pltff Tho Solemnly Called came not but made default nor in his Suit further prosecuted therefore it is ordered by the Court that the Plaintiff be non Suited and that the Defendant go hence without day and recover of the Plaintiff his Costs by him about his ~~suit~~ Defence in this behalf expended.

| | |
|---|---|
| James Wiley | Plaintiff |
| vs | |
| Lewis Evans | Defendant |

By Consent of the Parties it is ordered that this Suit be continued till the next Court.

---

| | |
|---|---|
| Jonathan Davis | Plaintiff |
| vs | In /Blank/ |
| Ezekiel Vansant | Defendant |

This day came the parties by their attornies and there upon came a Jury to wit, Nathan Sawyze, Gideon Hopkins, James West, John Boles, George Killian, John Armstreet, Archabald Evans, Christopher Harmon, Jesse Bell, Bennett Truly, Moses Moore ~~George Killian~~ Joseph Killian who being elected tried and Sworn well and truly to try the Issue Joined upon their oath do say the the Defendant is Guilty in Manner and form as the Plaintiff against him hath declared in his Declaration and they do assess the plaintiff Damages by occasion thereof to one Cent besides his costs Therefore it is Considered by the Court that the plaintiff recover against the Said Deft$^s$ his Damages aforesaid in Manner and form by the Jurors in their Verdict aforesaid assessed and also his costs by him about his suit in this behalf expended and the Said Defendant in Mercy &$^c$ which Said Damages and costs in the whole make.

Moses Moore, foreman

| | |
|---|---|
| Abijah Hunt | Plaintiff |
| vs | in /Blank/ |
| Benjamine Kitchens | Defendant |

By consent of the parties by their attornies it is Ordered this Suit be dismissed at Defendants Costs.

---

In pursuance of an Act of Asembly for that purpose the Court proceeded to nominate the number of Jurors for this County as directed by the Said act to attend at the next Superior Court for the District of of Adams, Whereupon the following house keepers and freeholders were nominated to wit, Joseph Pannell, Israel Smith, Isaac Gilliard,

William Williams, Anthony Hoggatt, Jacob Earhart, Gabriel Swayze, David Allison, Daniel Whitaker, Elijah Eastis, Anthony Dougherty, Samuel Lusk, Abner Buckham, John Irwin, Absalom Griffin, Benjamine Darcy David Ferguson, Jonathan Dayton, William Brooks, John McCoy, John Bradley, Joseph Declarmount, Robert Childress, Nathaniel Tomlinson, Ezekiel Dewitt, Bennett Truly, Samuel Timberlake, James McIntosh, Robert Moore, Thomas Grafton, William Barland & William McIntosh it is ordered that a writ of Venire facias Issue to the Sheriff accordingly.
    Court adjourned for one hour.

                              Court according to adjournment met
                                      Present
                                      Samuel Brooks
                                      Ferdinand L. Claiborne
                                      James Neilson   Esquires
                                      Jonathan Guice
                                      Joseph Erwin

    David Gibson Exhibited an account in Court against the County of Adams amounting to twenty Dollars and fifty Cents which being examined was allowed was ordered to be certified.

---

    On the motion of Benjamine Seamans Clerk of the Court, Samuel May is admited as his deputy who thereupon took the usual oath of office and the oath to support the Constitution of the United States.

| | | | |
|---|---|---|---|
| Duncan | Francisway Augustin | | Plaintiff |
| | vs | | in /Blank/ |
| | Wilford Hoggatt | | Defendant |

On Motion of the Plaintiff, by his Attorney, it is ordered that the suit be dismissed at the Costs of the Plaintiff's attorney, to wit, Abner L. Duncan.
    Benjamine Holmes and John Irwin Esquires Returned an appraisment of a Stray Sorrel Horse taken up by Abner Buckham of this County and the same is ordered to be Recorded in the Record Book for Recording Strays and that a true Copy be posted at the door of the Courthouse two terms Successively and published three times in the Public Newspapers
                                              Absent
                                              Joseph Irwin Esq.

| | | |
|---|---|---|
| Bra | William Brooks | Plaintiff |
| | vs | |
| Wallace | Barton Harmon | Defendant |

On the Motion of the plaintiff by his attorney it is ordered that the Suit be Dismissed.

---

| | | |
|---|---|---|
| Har | John Conner | Plaintiff |
| Reed | Vs | In /Blank/ |
| Wal | Patrick Connally | Defendant |

This day came the parties by their attornies and thereupon came a Jury to witt Nathan Swayze, Gideon Hopkins, James West, John Bolls, George

(156-158)

Killian, John Armstreet, Archibald Evans, Christopher Harmon, Jesse Bell Bennet Truly, Moses Moore, & Joseph Killian who being elected tried and Sworn well and truly to try the Issue Joined upon their Oath do Say that the Defendant did assume upon himself in Manner and form as the Plaintiff against him hath declared and they do assess the plaintiff Damages by reason thereof to one hundred and thirty six Dollars and ninety Cents besides Costs therefore it is Considered by the Court that the Plaintiff recover against the Said Defendant his Damages aforesaid in Manner and form by the Jurors in their verdict aforesaid assessed and also his costs by him about his suit in this behalf expended and the Said Defendant in Mercy &c

John Wells      Plaintiff
Vs         Notice in Sale Sheriff
William Brooks     Defendant

the Plaintiff by his attorney, /Blank/ the Court that this notice be continued till Saturday next

   The Court adjourned till tomorrow Morning 9 o'clock

---

157

       Court agreeable to Adjournment met
       Oct. 7th
         Present
          Saml Brooks
          William Darby   Esquires
          Joseph Irwin
          Jonathan Guice

Dun   David Ferguson     Plt
    vs          Case   Rule Reference
Mahn   David Harvard     Deft

This day came the parties by their attornies and agree to refer this suit to the determination To Joseph Harmon and David Gibson to Report as of this Term with Stay of execution three months the Disposition of Benjamine Pain to taken before James Neilson Esquire on four Days notice and Read in Evedience.

Mah    Jonathan Davis     Plaintiff
Poindexter   vs         Case
&     Ezekiel Vanet      Defendant
Wallace

This day came the Plaintiff by his Said attorney and moved the Court that the Judgment obtained yesterday may be set and the ~~Plaintiff set in cost of Judgt~~ on the ~~Jurers verdict en this cause being argued the Court was of opinion that there is no sufficient ground for a new trial may be stayd be made &c~~ & prays that the Judgt on the Verdict aforesaid be Stayed.

---

158

  Ordered by the Court that No Judgment by default Judgment on non Pros or non Suit shall be entered unless the party against whom such

Judgment non Pros on non Suit is to be entered by first openly and Solemnly called to appear and answer or prosecute as the case may be.

| | | |
|---|---|---|
| Har | Lewis Evans | Plaintiff |
| | vs | in Debt |
| Dun | Ebenezer Rees | Defendant |

This day came the parties by their attornies and the Defendant by his attorney Waving his former Plea Says he cannot gain say the Plaintiff's Action against him therefore it is considered by the Court that the Plaintiff recover against the Said Def$^t$ the Sum of his costs by him about his Suit in this behalf expended and and also the Said Defendant in Mercy &$^c$ the Plaintiff agree to Stay the execution of this Judgment till next term.

| | | |
|---|---|---|
| Wheatly | Rouben Kemper | Plaintiff |
| Recorder | vs | In Case |
| Har | James Wilkins | Defendant |

This day came the parties by their attornies and the Def$^t$ by his attorney Waving his former Plea says he cannot gain Say the plaintiff's Action against him therefore it is Considered by the Court that the plaintiff recover against the Said Defendant the the sum of fifty Dollars besides his Costs of Suit and the plaintiff by his Said attorney agrees to stay the execution of the Judgment till next term.

---

| | | |
|---|---|---|
| Har | St James Beauvies | Plaintiff |
| Recorded | vs | Case |
| Wal | Patrick Connally | Defendant |

This day came the parties by their attornies and the Said Defendant comes into Court in his proper person and the Said Defendant acknowledges the plaintiff's Action therefore is is Considered by the court that the plaintiff recover against the said Defendant the sum of one hundred and six Dollars and Seventy eight cents also his costs by him about his suit in this behalf expended and the Said Defendant in Mercy &$^c$ and the Plaintiff by his Att$^o$ agrees to Stay execution of this Judgment till first of February next.

| | | |
|---|---|---|
| | A. Hunt | Plaintiff |
| | vs | in Case | Reed's Death |
| | Patrick Connally & Thomas Reed | Defendant | suggested |

This day came the parties by their attorneys and thereupon came a Jury to wit, Gideon Hopkins, James West, John Bells, George, Killian, Moses Moore, Philip Hoggatt, John Armstreet, Archibald Evans, Christopher Harmon, Jesse Bell, Nathan Swayze, and Joseph Killian who being elected tried and Sworn well and truly to try the Issue Joined upon their oath do Say that the Deft$^s$ Did assume in Manner and form as the plaintiff against them in his Declaration hath declared and do assess the Plaintiff damages by reason thereof to fifty five Dollars besides costs therefore it is considered by the court that the Plaintiff recover against the said Defendant his damages aforesaid in Manner and form by the Jurors in their verdict aforesaid assessed and also his Costs by him about his Suit in this behalf expended & the Defendant in Mercy &$^c$

Moses Moore, foreman

## Present John Henderson Esq[r]

| | | |
|---|---|---|
| Dun | Robert Moore | Plaintiff |
| Recorded | Vs | Case |
| Wal | Charles Dowling | Defendant |

This day came the parties by their attorneys and the Defendant by his attorney waving his former Plea and Saving and reserving to himself every advantage he may have in Equity Says he cannot gain Say the plaintiff's action against him therefore it is considered by the Court that the plaintiff recover against the Said Defendant fifty five Dollars and one eighth of a hundred Cents and also his Costs by him about his Suit in this behalf expended and the Said Defendant in Mercy &c and the Plaintiff agrees to Stay execution of this Judgment till the first of Feb[ry] next.

| | | |
|---|---|---|
| Har | William Kenner | Plaintiff |
| Recorded | Vs | in Case |
| Mah | Luke Whiting | Defendant |

This day came the parties by their attorneys and the Said Defendant waving his former plea say he connot gain say the plaintiff's action against him Therefore it is Considered by the Court that the plaintiff recover against the Said Defendant the Sum of thirty five Dollars & ninety Six Cents also his costs by him about his Suit in this behalf expended and the Said Defendant in Mercy &c

---

| | | | |
|---|---|---|---|
| Bra | Ext[ors] Morris Stackpool | Plaintiff | |
| | Vs | in Case | |
| Har | William B. Smith | Defendant | Rule Referance |

This day came the parties by their Attornies and agree to Submit all Matters in difference betwen them to the final Determination of Love Baker and Henry Turner and their Report be Retained in Office made the Judgment of the Court and execution to Issue thereon.

| | | |
|---|---|---|
| Har | St James Beauvies | Plaintiff |
| Recorded | Vs | in Debt |
| Wal | David Johnston | Defendant |

This day came the parties by their attorneys and the Said defendant by his attorney waving his former plea Says he cannot gain Say the plaintiff's action against him thr[e]fore it is considered by the Court that the plaintiff recover against the Said Defendant.

---

| | | |
|---|---|---|
| G.P.Wal | Ezra Johns | Plt |
| | Vs | Attachment |
| Calvit | Amos Hubbard | Deft |

On Motion of W[m] Smith by the Defendants attorney it is ordered by the Court that an interpleader be filed by the Said Smith in this Suit.

    Court adjourned till 9 O'clock.

(162-163)

Court agreeable to adjournment met
Present
Samuel Brooks
Jonathan Guice    Esquires
Joseph Irwin

|  | George Killian | Plaintiff |
|  | vs | Attachment |
|  | George Lownig | Defendant |

Joseph Killian Garnishee being Sworn made oath he stands indetted to the defendant in the Sum of two hundred Dollars whereupon it is ordered by the Court that the Said Joseph retain in his hands the Sum of Sixty Doll$^s$ a part of the Said Debt till the further order of this Court.

Bra
Recorded     Asa Searcy           Plt
Mah          vs                   in Debt
             Stephen Stephenson   Def$^t$

This day came the parties by their attornies and the Said Def$^t$ Relinquishing his former plea Says he cannot gain Say the plaintiff's action against him therefore it is Considered by the Court that the plaintiff recover against the Said Defendant Seventy eight Dollars and fifty cents and also his Costs in this behalf expended and the Def$^t$ in Mercy. Stay Ex$^{cton}$ till the first March.

163

Wal     James Wiley         Plaintiff
        vs                  in /Blank/
Har     Lewis Evans         Defendant

On the the motion of the Motion of the Plaintiff by his attorney it is ordered that this Suit be continued till the next term.

B.L.Hur  Abijah Hunt        Plaintiff
         vs                 in Case
Wal      Peter Anthony      Defendant

By consent of the parties it is ordered that this suit be continued till the next Court.

         Benjamin Kitchens  Plt
         vs                 in Case      Rule of Ref$^e$
         Bryan Bruin        Def$^t$      Set aside

The former Rule not being performed is Discharged whereupon came the parties by their Said Attornies and and thereupon came a Jury to wit, Nathan Swayze, Jun$^r$, Gideon Hopkins, James West, John Bolls, John Armstreet, Archibald Evans, Christian Harmon, Jesse Bell, Joseph Killian, George Killian, Nathan Swayze, Son$^r$, and Moses Moore, who being elected tried and Sworn well and truly to try the Issue Joined ~~Who being elected tried and Sworn well and truly to try the Issue Joined~~ upon their oath do say that the Defendant did assume in Manner and form at the plaintiff forty six Dollars and fifty Cents Damages besides Costs therefore it is considered by the Court that the Plaintiff recover against the Said Defendant his damages aforesaid in Manner by the Jurors in In their verdict aforesaid assessed and also his Costs by him about his Suit in this behalf expended and which in the whole make and the Defendant in Mercy &$^c$

Claiborn Boles made oath that he attended in the Suit Benjamin Kitchens vs Brian Bruin one day as a witness therefore is entitled to the allowance by Law to wit One Dollar.

Court adjourned till tomorrow 9 O'clock.

Court agreeable to adjournment met Saturday 8$^{th}$ 1803

Present
Sam$^l$ Brooks
John Henderson Esquire
Jonathan Guice

Har     Fielding Denny     Plt
          vs           in Case
Val     Price & Whiting     Def$^t$

This day came the parties by their attornies and the Said Def$^{ts}$ by his said attorney waving his former Plea Says they cannot Gainsay the Plaintiff's action against them therefore it is considered by the Court that the Plaintiff recover against the Said defendants eighty five Dollars and eighty four Cents and also his Costs by them about his Suit in this behalf expended and the Said Defendant in Mercy &$^c$ and the plaintiff agrees to Stay execution of this Judg$^t$ till the first of January next.

---

Dun     Stephen Odair     Plaintiff
          vs           in Case
Muncy     Ann Martin     Defendant

On the motion of the Plaintiff by his attorney it is ordered that this Suit be continued till next Court.

Dun     Ex$^{tors}$ William Vousdan     Pltff$^s$
          vs           Case     Annaboll Smith
Bra     Morris Stackpooles Ex$^{tors}$     Def$^{ts}$

the Parties by their Attorneys agree the Ex$^{tors}$ appear without Citation.

Wal     Patrick and T. Campbell     Pltffs
          Vs           Appeal from Justice
          Esox Capshaw     Def$^t$

This day came the plaintiffs by their attornies and the Def$^t$ in his Proper Person and the Said Defendant acknowledges the Plaintiff's action, therefore it is considered by the Court that the plaintiff recover against the Said Defendant nineteen Dollars and fifty four and also the costs by him about their suit in this behalf expended and the Said Defendant in Mercy &$^c$ and the Plaintiffs agree to stay the Execution of the Judgment till the first of January next.

Wal     The Same     Pltffs.
          Vs           Same
          The Same     Def$^t$

The the same above for eleven dollars and Costs with Stay of Execution till the first January next.

| | | |
|---|---|---|
| Bra | Asey Searcy | Pltff |
| Recorded | vs | in Debt |
| Mahan | Barton Harmon | Deft |

This day came the parties by their attorneys and the Defendants by this Said attorney Relinquishing his former Plea and Saving and Reserving to himself every advantage he may have in equity says he cannot gainsay the plaintiff's action against him, therefore it is Considered by the Court that the Plaintiff recover against the Said Defendant Sixty two Dollars with interest thereon to to be computed at the Rate of five percentum Per Annum till paid and also his Costs by him about his Suit in this behalf expended which in the whole make Seventy Seven Dollars & Seventy Cents and the Said Defendant in Mercy &c & the Plaintiff agrees to Stay execution till first February next.

Court adjourned till half after 9 O'clock.

Court agreeable to Adjt met
Present
Samuel Brooks
John Henderson    Esquires
&
William Darby

| | | | |
|---|---|---|---|
| | Benjamine Kitchens | Plt | |
| | vs | in Case | |
| | Bryan Bruin | Deft | Judgt by Jury for Plt |

The Defendant by his attorney Prayed an appeal to the next Superior Court of Law to be holden for the District of Adams which is granted with the condition the Said Defendant do give Robert Cockran as Security in Said appeal to be conditioned according to Law.

---

| | | |
|---|---|---|
| Bra | David Ferguson | Plaintiff |
| | vs | Debt |
| Mah | Christopher Lee | Defendant |

This day came the Parties by their Attorneys and the Said Defendant by his attorney acknowledges the Plaintiff's action, therefore it is considered by the Court that the Plaintiff Recover against the Defendant Eighty three Dollars and fifty Cents and interest thereon from the date of the note at five prCent and also his Costs by him about his Suit in this behalf expended and the said Defendant in Mercy &c and the plaintiff agrees to Stay the execution of the Judgment till the first of February next.

This Suit was droped on the dockett.

| | | |
|---|---|---|
| Mah | John Duhamil | Pltff |
| Recorded | vs | in Debt |
| Har | Samuel Hindman | Deft |

This day came the parties by their attornies and the Defendant by his Said attorney Relinquishing his former plea and Saving and Reserving every advantage he may have in equity Says he cannot gainsay the plaintiff's action against him, therefore it is considered by the court that the plaintiff Recover against the the Said Defendant Sixty Dollars the Debt in the declaration mentioned and Legal interest thereon and also his Costs by him about his suit in this behalf expended which in the whole make Seventy Seven Dollars & ten cents and the Said Defendant in Mercy &c

| | | |
|---|---|---|
| Debt | 60 | " |
| Interest | 7 | " |
| Costs | 10 | 10 |

Dun    Thomas House               Pltff
Recorded    vs                        in Debt
Mah    David Havard              Def$^t$

This day came the parties by their attornies and the Defendant by his said attorney acknowledges the plaintiff's action ag$^t$ him. Therefore it is Considered by the Court that the plaintiff recover against the Said Defendant twenty two Dollars, the Debt in the Dec$^l$. Mentioned, also four Dollars twelve and one half cents Damages for the Detention of the Same besides Costs which in the whole make thirty Six Dollars twelve & half cents and the Defendant in Mercy &$^c$

Debt      $22
Dam      4 12½    $36 12½
Costs    10

Wal    John Wells               Plaintiff
Recorded    vs                        in Notice
        William Brooks late Sheriff    Defendant

This day came the plaintiff by his attorney and the Def$^t$ failing to appear whereupon by the Consent of the plaintiff by his Counsel this motion is Continued till Thursday next.

Wal    Jacob Stagel              Plaintiff
        vs                        in Case
        Ezra Johns              Defendant

Abates by death of the Defendant.

Har    Charles Surget             Plaintiff
        vs                        case
        Elisha Adams             Defendant

By Consent it is ordered that this Suit be Dismissed.

        St James Beauvais         Plaintiff
        vs                        in Case
        George Lawing            Def$^t$

On Motion of the Pltffs Att$^o$. this suit is Continued till next court.

---

Har    William Darby              Plaintiff
        vs                        in Cove
        William Johnston         Defendant

On the Motion of the plaintiff by his attorney ordered that his suit be dismissed.

(169-170)

| | | |
|---|---|---|
| Har | Thomas Irwin | Pltff |
| Deft for | Vs | In Case |
| costs | Martin McCullock | Defendant |

This day came the parties by their attornies and the Defendant by his Said attorney relinquishes his former plea acknowledges the plaintiff's action therefore it is considered by the Court that Plaintiff recover against the Said Defendant thirty three Dollars and also his costs by him about his suit in this behalf expended which in the whole makes forty three and Sixty Cents and the said Defendant in Mercy &c and the plaintiff agrees to Stay the Execution of this Judg$^t$ till next term.

| | | |
|---|---|---|
| Dun | Moores Exto$^{rs}$ | Plaintiff |
| | Vs | Case |
| | John Tally | Defendant |

This day came the Plaintiff by his attorney and the Def$^t$ being Solemnly called came not but made default, therefore it considered by the Court that the Plaintiff recover against the Said Defendant his damages Sustained by occasion of the Defendant's non Performance of the promises and assumption in the Declaration Mentioned and because it is not known what Damages the Plt hath Sustained it is ordered that the same be enquired of and assessed by a Jury at the next Court.

170

| | | |
|---|---|---|
| Mch | Patrick Connally | Plaintiff |
| Wal | Vs | Case |
| Tur | John Shackler | Defendant |
| Braz | | |
| Recorded | | |

This day came the parties by their Attornies and thereupon came a Jury to wit, Nathan Swayze, James West, Gideon Hopkins, John Bells, George Killion, John Armstreet, Archibald Evans, Christian Harmon, Moses Moore, John Barney, Moses Kiddy & Walter McCloland, who being elected tried and Sworn well and truly to try the Issue Joined Retired to consider of the verdict and after sometime returned and reported they Could not agree whereupon by consent of the parties and with the assent of the Court Moses Moore one of the Jurors aforesaid was withdrawn and the rest of the Jurors from Rendering their verdict are Discharged and the parties by their Said attornies agree that this Cause be taken to the Superior Court as on an appeal and then entered at the next term and that commissions may be Issued by the Clerk of the Said Supreme Court at any time hereafter to such commissioner or commissioners as he may appoint to take the Depositions of Absent witnesses or Interrogaltories the party applying for such didimas giving the oposite party ten Days notice of the time of Issuing thereof together with a Copy of his interrogatories.

 Court adjourned till Monday 9 O'clock.

       Monday Oct 10 Court agreeable to adjournment Met.
         Present
          Samuel Brooks, Esquire
       Ordered Court be adjourned till tomorrow morning nine o'clock.

James Griffin presented in Court an account against the County which being examined is allowed and ordered to be Certified of

|  |  |
|---|---|
| | $24.62$\frac{1}{2}$ |
| Antoni Figaro Same of | 16.50 |
| Ferdinand Claiborne Same of | 130.87$\frac{1}{2}$ |
| Christopher Lee Same | 33.50 |
| | $205.50 |

Robert Bashford presented an acounty against the County which being examined by the Court is laidover for further Consideration whereupon the Court Proceeded to allow one hundred and fifty Dollars to be certified to the auditor of of public accounts and the Said one hundred and fifty Doll$^{rs}$ to be deducted from the Said Bashfords account when hereafter examined.

William Nicholls Presented an account of Eighty Six dollars and ninety cents to here think proper to Submit it to the opinion of the Attorney General the Same becomes a Territorial or County Charge.

Court adjourned till tomorrow 9 o'clock

Sam$^l$ Brooks C. J.
Court met agreeable to adjournment
Wednesday 13th 1803
Present
Samuel Brooks
John Henderson    Esquires
&
John Foster

Wal Robert Willson   Plt
  vs       in Case
Har John Sweaney   Deft

This day came the Defendant by his Attorney and the Pltff tho Solemnly called came not but made Default nor is his Suit further prosecuted therefore on the Prayer of the Defendant by his said Attorney it is ordered by the Court the Plaintiff be non Suited and the Defendant go hence without day and Receive of the Plaintiff his Costs by him about his Defence in this behalf expended.

Har James Beauvais & Co  Plt
Recorded vs       in Case
Dft John Cammock   Deft

This day came the parties by their attorneys and the Said Defendant by his said attorney Relinquishing his former Plea Says he cannot gainsay the Plaintiff's action against him therefore it is considered by the court that the plaintiff recover against the Said Defendant Eighty eight dollars and seven cents and also his costs by him about his suit in this behalf expended and the Said Defend$^t$ in Mercy &c and the plaintiff agrees to Stay execution of this Judgment three months.

  George Rapalie   Plt
  vs       in Trover
  Elijah Loyd    Deft

This day came the Parties by their attornies and agree that the former Rule of Reference made herein be continued.

(172-174)

| Har | William Thompson | Pl$^t$ |
|---|---|---|
| | vs | in Case |
| Mah | Rowland Shackelford | Def$^t$ |

With consent of the parties by their attornie it is ordered this suit be continued till the next Court.

---

173

| Dfts | John Perkins | Pl$^t$ |
|---|---|---|
| Recorded | vs | in Case |
| Wal | Patrick Connally | Def$^t$ |

This day came the Parties by their attornies and thereupon came a Jury to wit, John Bolls, George Killian, Christopher Harmon, Jesse Bell, John Burney, Bonnet Truly, Samuel Timberlake, Joseph Strickland, Thomas Harris, John Campbell, Moses Kiddy & John Overaker who being elected tried and sworn well and truly to try the Issue Joined upon their oath do say that the Defendant did assume upon himself in Manner and form as the plaintiff in his declaration against him hath Declared and do assess the plaintiff Damages by Reason thereof To one Hundred and Seventy Dollars and Sixty Seven Cents besides Costs, therefore it is considered by the Court that the Plaintiff recover against the said Defendant his Damages aforesaid assessed and also his costs by him about his Suit in this behalf expended which in the whole make one hundred and eighty Dollars & sixty seven Cents, and the Said Defendant in Mercy &$^c$

```
Dam      170.67
Costs     10       180.67
```

| Wal | Lewis Moore | Pl$^{ts}$ |
|---|---|---|
| Recorded | vs | Case |
| Har | George Sheras | Defend$^t$ |

This day came the parties by their Attornies and the Said Defendant by his attorney relinquishing his former plea acknowledges the plaintiff's action therefore it is Considered by the Court that the plaintiff recover fifty six Dollars eighty Seven & one half cents and also his costs by him about his Suit in this behalf expended and the Said Defendant in Mercy &$^c$ and the Plaintiff agrees to stay Ex$^{on}$ till the first of Jan$^{ry}$ Lewis Moore the plaintiff acknowledges to have Rec$^d$ of Sam$^l$ Mahan the Def$^{ts}$ Bail the amt of this Judg$^t$

November 1804, S. May

---

174

| Dunlop | Samuel Null | Pl$^t$ |
|---|---|---|
| Recorded | vs | in Case |
| Wal | William Darby | Def$^t$ |

This day came the parties by their attornies and the Defendant by his Said attorney relinquishing his former plea, say he cannot Gainsay the Plaintiff's action against him therefore it is considered by the Court that the Plaintiff recover against the Said Defendant thirty four dollars Seventy Seven Cents and

also his cost by him about his suit in this behalf expended and the Said defendant in Mercy &c and the Plaintiff agrees to Stay the Execution of the Judgment till the first of January.
Court adj^d till two o'clock.

                                Court according to adjournment met
                                    Present
                                    Sam^l Brooks
                                    James Neilson
                                    Will^m Foster        Esq^rs
                                          &
                                    John Henderson

Dfs       John Perkins              Plt
Recorded     vs                     In Case
Wal       P. Connally & Clark       Deft

This day came the Parties by their attorneys and thereupon came a Jury to wit, John Bolls, Samuel Timberlake, Bennet Truly John Campbell, Joseph Strickland Jesse Bell, Moses Kiddy, Robert Bashford, George Killian, Christopher Harmon, Walter McCleland & Robe^t Patterson who being elected tried and Sworn well and truly to try the Issue Joined upon their oath do Say that the Defendant did assume upon himself in Manner and form as the plaintiff in his declaration against him hath declared and do assess the plaintiff Damages by Reason thereof to thrity Seven Dollars and Six Cents besided Costs therefore it is considered by the court that the Plaintiff recover against the Defendant

---

175

Damages aforesaid in Manner and form by the Jurors in their Verdict aforesaid assessed and also his Costs by him about his suit in this behalf expended which in the whole make forty Seven Dollars and six Cents and the Said Defendant in Mercy &c

Bra       Joseph Bell               Plaintiff
Recorded     vs                     In Case
Wal       Patrick Connally          Defendant

This day came the Parties by their attornies and the said Defendant by his attorney acknowledges the plaintiff's Action therefore it is considered by the Court that the plaintiff recover his costs by him about his suit in this behalf expended and the said Defendant in Mercy &c.

Har       John Irwin                Plt
Recorded     vs                     In Debt
Tur       Moses Moore               Deft

This day came the Parties by their attornies and the Defendant by his Said attorney Relinquishing his former Plea and Saving and Reserving to himself every to himself every advantage he may have in equity Says he cannot gainsay the Plaintiffs action against him therefore it is considered by the Court that the Plaintiff Recover against the Defendant Seven hundred and thirty four Dollars and eighty cents and also his Costs by him about his Suit in this behalf exponced and the Said Defendant in Mercy &c and the Plaintiff agrees to Stay Execution of this Judg^t till the first of March next.

176

| | | |
|---|---|---|
|Mah|Joseph Martinez|Plt|
| |vs|in Case|
| |David Kennady|Def^t|

Ordered that a Citation Issue to the Adm^ors to come forward and defend this Suit.

| | | |
|---|---|---|
| |Jonathan Davis|Plt|
| |vs|In Debt|
|Mah|John Whitton|Defendant|

This day came the plaintiff by his attorney and the Said Def^t not appearing tho Solemnly called upon the motion of the Plt by his attorney it is ordered that the plaintiff recover of the Defendant his Costs by him about his Suit in this behalf Expended and

| | | |
|---|---|---|
|Wal|John Holly|Plt|
| |vs|in Case|
|Df|John Campbell|Def^t|

This day came as well the Defendant by his attorney as the Plt by James his Atto and the Said Defendant prays & has leave to impart until the next Court and then to Plead.

| | | |
|---|---|---|
| |James Warren|Plt|
| |vs|in Case|
| |Thomas Ragen|Def^t|

By consent of the Parties it is ordered that this Suit be Con^d till next Court.

| | | |
|---|---|---|
|Wah|James Malson|Plt|
| |vs|in Case|
|Har|Benjamin Kitchen|Deft|

By consent of the Parties it is ordered that the former Rule of Reference made herein be continued.

---

177

| | | |
|---|---|---|
| |James Flannigan|Plt|
| |vs|in Cov^t|
| |Lewis Shelton|Deft|

This day this day came the Parties by their and the Defendant by his said attorney Relinquishing his former Plea and Saving and Reserving to himself every advantage he may have in Equity Says he cannot gainsay the Plttfs action against him, therefore it is considered by the court that the Plaintiff recover against the Said Defendant the Sum of twenty three Dollars thirty three and one third Cents Debt the Debt in the Declment and also nine Dollars and ten cents, his costs by him about his suit in this behalf expended and the Said Defendant in Mercy &^c & the plaintiff agrees to Stay the Execution of this Judg^t till the first of April next.

Certified  James Neilson Esquire Produced in Court an account against the County of Adams which being examined was allowed & ordered to be certified for $37.50.

| | | |
|---|---|---|
|Har|Ferguson & Woolley|Plttf|
|Recorded|vs|in Case|
|Dps|William McWilliams|Deft|

This day came the parties by their attornies and the Deft by his Said attorney Relinquishing his former plea acknowledges the plaintiffs action therefore it is considered by the Court that the plaintiff Recover of the

Said Defendant fifty six Dollars and also his costs by him about his suit in this behalf expended and the Defendant in Mercy &c and the Plaintiff agrees to stay the Execution of this Judgment till the first of March next.

---

178

   Moore Ex$^{tors}$     Plts
     vs        in Case
   Winneford Payne    Deft

On the Motion of the Plaintiff by his attorney it is ordered that this Suit be dismissed.

Dun  Anthony Grass     Plaintiff
     vs        Case
Drp  Margaret Barton Ad$^{tor}$  Defendant

This day came the parties by their attornies that amendment be made on Both sides and then to plead.

Dun  Es$^{tors}$ of W. Moore   Plt
     vs        in Case
Wal  Willis Benner Ad$^{mr}$   Deft

By consent of parties by their Attornies it is ordered that this Suit be dismissed.

Wal  Thomas Munfield    Plttfs
     vs        Attachment
Mah  David McCleland    Deft

The Parties by their attornies and agree to that the deposition of Absent Witnesses be taken agreeable to the former order made herein at the last Court be continued and that a Didimus Issue accordingly.

Dun  Phillip Alston Jun$^{r}$   Plt
     vs        case
   Eunice McIntosh    Deft

To be taken by consent of the Parties to the Supreme Court.

   The Same       Pltff
     vs        Case
   The Same       Deft   The Same

---

179

Dun  Moore Ex$^{tors}$     Plt
     vs        Case
Har  Richard King Ex$^{tors}$   Deft

The Defendant by his Said attorney and prays leave to Impart till the next Court and then to Plead which is granted him under a Particular Rule for trial at the next Court.

Wallace  John E. Long    Plt
     vs        Case
Duncan  George Rapalie    Deft

The Parties by their attornies agree and it is ordered that this cause be continued till the next court.

Har    Panton Loftes & Co.   Plt
Recorded   vs       in Case
Dun    Bryan Bruin     Deft

This day came the parties by their attornies and thereupon came a Jury to wit, John Bells, Samuel Timberlake, Bennet Truly, John Campbell, Joseph

(179-181)

Strickland, Jesse Bell, and Moses Kiddy, Robert Bashford, George Killian, Christopher Harmon, Walter McCleland & Robert Patterson, who being elected tried and Sworn well and truly to try the Issue Joined upon their oath do do say that the plaintiff do assume upon himself in Manner and form as the Plaintiff in his declaration against him hath Declared and to assess the Plaintiff damages by Reason thereof to two hundred and thirty three Dollars damages besides costs therefore it is considered by the Court that the plaintiff Recover of the Defendant his damages aforesaid in Manner and form by the Jurors in their verdict aforesaid assessed and also his Costs by him about his Suit in this behalf expended which in the whole make and the Said Defendant in Mercy &c

180

Ker     Robert Park     Plt
           vs     In Debt
Mah     James Malson     Deft

This day came the Parties by their attornies and the Defendant by his said attorney relinquishing his former Plea and Saving & Reserving to himself every advantage he may have in Equity Says he cannot gainsay the plaintiffs action against him therefore it is Considered by the Court that the plaintiff Recover against the Said Defendant fifty Dollars the Debt in the declaration mentioned and six Dollars Damages besides Costs which in the whole makes [Blank] and the Said Defendant in Mercy &c

Ker     Culberson Parks     Pltt
           vs     In Case
Mah     James Malson     Deft

By consent of parties ordered that this Suit be continued to take Depositions.

Dp     United States     Plt
Recorded     vs     In Deby
           Hogg & Thery     Deft     Amecable Suit

This day came the United States by James Dunlop the Att$^o$ in that behalf and the Defendant in Proper Person and the Defendant acknowledges the Pltffs action thereford it is considered by the Court that the plaintiff recover of the Defendant the Debt in the Declaration mentioned and also his Costs by him about his suit in this behalf expended and the Said Defendant in Mercy &c

181

Dp     United States     Pltff
Recorded     vs     In Debt
Mahan     James Hogg & I. B. Theri     Def     Amicable Suit

This day came as Well James Dunlop Esquire attorney in behalf of the United States and the Defendant in Proper Person and the Said Defendant acknowledges the plaintiff's action therefore it is considered by the court that the plaintiff recover against the said Defendant the Debt in the Declaration mentioned and also his Costs by him about his suit in this behalf expended and the Said Defendant in Mercy &c

Dp Recorded
William Dunbar Junr Plt
vs in Debt
James Wallace Deft

This day came the Plaintiff by his attorney and the Deft in Proper Person and the Said Defendant acknowledges the Plaintiffs action therefore it is considered by the Court that the Plaintiff recover against the said Defendant Seventy Dollars with stay of Execution until the first day of May and the Debt in Mercy &c the plaintiff agrees to pay all Cost ordered on the above Suit.

Abijah Hunt Plt
vs Case
Michael Moore Deft

Abates by the Death of the Defendant.

Ann Martin who made oath she attended Seven Days as a witness in the suit John Ferguson against David Havard therefore is entitled to the allowance made by Law to wit Seven Dollars.

---

John Burney & Thomas Harris being summonsed to attend this Court as Jurymen this day were Solemnly called but came not therefore it is ordered by the Court that for This contempt therein they Severally make their fine to his Excellency William C. C. Clairborn Governor of this Territory by the payment of two dollars Each for the use of the Territory and may be taken &c Whereupon Thos Harris came into Court and paid his fine aforesaid.

John Wells Plt
vs Notice
William Brooks late Sheriff Deft

This day came the Pltff by his attorney and the Present Sheriff of this County having returned that he served a copy of this notice on the defendant whereupon on the motion of the Plaintiff by his Counsel it ordered by the court that the plaintiff have Judgt vs the Defendant for the sum of one hundred and thirty six Dollars and twenty five cents, money made on a venditione esponas at this Suit of Said Wells vs John Holland and also the costs assured on this notice expended and the Said Deft in Mercy &c.

Ordered that Court be adjd till tomorrow 9 o'clock.

---

Court According to adjt met Thursday 14th 1803

Present
Samuel Brooks
John Henderson    Esqurs
William Foster

(183-185)

Benjamine Kitchens ad sectam Leonard Claiborn agreeable to a Writ directed from the Judges of the Superior Courts it is ordered that the Clerk of the County Court send an Authenticated Copy of the Proceedings with the writ so so directed to the next Superior Court of Law to be held for the said Defendant.

  Thomas Ervin        Pltiff
    Vs           in Case
  Smith & Kemper       Deft

By consent of the Parties it is ordered by the Court that this Suit be continued under the Rule for taking the deposition of witnesses on Interrogations ten days notice thereof being given to the oposite party.

  Samuel Brooks makes oath that he has attended ten days as a witness in the Suit, Patrick Connally vs Ezekiel Tileot he is therefore entitled to ten Dollars from the Plaintiff.

  William Thompson      Pltffs
    vs           in Trover
  Stephen Douglass       Defendant

  Samuel Brooks makes Oath that he has attended two days as a witness for the defendant he is therefore entitled to two Dollars.

---

184

Dp    J. P. Perkins        Pltff
      vs           in [Blank]
Wal    Connally & Clark      Deft

John Henderson Esquire makes oath that he has attended ten days as a witness for the Plaintiff therefore he is entitled to ten Dollars.

Har    William Kenner       Plt
      Vs           On attachment
    George Lawnig       Deft
    Bennett Truly        Plaintiff
      vs           Atta
    Same           Defendant

Ordered that the property attached in the above suits be Sold according to the Law in Such case made and Provided and Sold as Perishable Property.

Certified    Wm Nicholls produced in Court an account ag$^{st}$ the County for forty Dollars and Sixty five cents which being examined was allowed and ordered to be certified.

---

185

Certified    William Nicholls produced in Court an account against the County of Adams which being examined is allowed and ordered to be certified to the Auditor of Public Accounts for forty Dollars and Sixty five Cents $40.65

Wal    Benjamine Robinson    Plt
      vs           in Case
Dun Wh   Bennette Truly       Defendant

(185-186)

Ordered by the Court with Assent of the Parties that that commissions Issue to take the diposition of witnesses Residing in the Spanish Government in behalf of either of the Parties, Said Deposition to be taken on interrogations a copy of which shall be served on the Adverse Party or his attorney at least ten days Previous to the Isuing of Said Commission Saving Just exceptions to the Compitency or credibility of Said witnesses commissions to be app$^d$ by Samuel Brooks Esquire.

| | | |
|---|---|---|
| Har | Panton Laslie & Co. | Pltff |
| Recorded | vs | in Case |
| Dun | Bryan Bruin | Deft |

Judg$^t$ given heretofore

The Defendant by his attorney prayed an appeal from the Judg$^t$ in the Suit to the next Superior Court of Law to be holden for the district of Adams which is granted & the Parties agree that the appeal Bond to be taken out of Court provided the Said Defendant give Robert Cochran and one other free holder as Security within ten Days from the Rising of the Court or otherwise Execution to Issue thereon against the Defendant under the Penalty of four hundred and Sixty Six Dollars.

Ordered Court to adj$^d$ till Court in Course

Sam$^l$ Brooks J. P.

---

186

At a County Court held for the County of Adams at the Courthouse thereof in the City of Natchez on Monday the fifth Day of December 1803
Present
Samuel Brooks      Esquires
John Henderson

Ordered that Court be adjourned till tomorrow Morning nine O'clock.
Tuesday the 6th 1803, Court agreeable to adj$^t$ Met.
Present
John Henderson  Esqr.

Ordered that Court be adjourned till tomorrow Morning 9 o'clock for want of a Sufficient Corum.

Wednesday 7$^{th}$ 1803, Court Met accg$^r$ to adj met
Present
Samuel Brooks
&        Esquires
John Henderson

Ordered that Court be adjourned till tomorrow morning 9 o'clock for want of Sufficient Corum.

Thursday 8$^{th}$ 1803, Court according to adjourment met
Present
Sam$^l$ Brooks
John Callender &    Esquires
W$^m$ Foster

| | |
|---|---|
| United States | Plaintiff |
| vs | In Debt |
| James & Robert Moore | Defendant |
| Same | Plaintiff |
| vs | Same |
| Same 2$^d$ Suit | Defendant |
| Same | Plaintiff |
| vs | Same |
| Same 3$^d$ | Defendant /Blank/ |

in the above suits the Writs Returned to this Term to Wit September the Parties agree that Clerks Issue against the Said Defendant's in three Suits the Said Defendants not to be charged with the costs of the first Original Writ.

In pursuance of an act of assembly for that purpose the Court proceeded to nominate the number of Jurors for this County as directed by the Said act to attend at the next Superior Court for the District of Adams Whereupon the following housekeepers and freeholders were nominated to wit, Walter Burling, Charles Surget, Joshua Howard Jun$^r$, William Hoggatt, Thomas Foster, Isaac Guion, Richard King, David Killian, Thomas Wilkins, William Dunbar Jun$^r$. James Dunbar, Robert Parkison, William Cochran, Adam Bingamin, David Holt, Andrew Walker, James Foster, Nathan Hoggatt, Calvin Smith, Gabriel Swayze, Elisha Estis, Abner Bockham, James McIntosh Samuel Watson, John Grafton, Richard Sessions & John T. Taylor and it is ordered a Venire facias Issue according.

---

Certified   William Nicholls Sheriff produced in Court an account of nine Dollars eighteen and three fourth Cents which being examined is allowed and ordered to be certified.           $9.18-3/4.

Benjamine Seamans Clerk of this Court produced in Court an account against the County for Certain Services Rendered Said County to wit, Recording the annual returns made by the Matistrates of 3$^d$ County and furnishing five Different Copies & taking bond given by the Sheriff & Recording the Same the Court the Court have allowed at the rate of Sixteen Cents per sheet for the original list and twelve and one half cents for every hundred words, copies thereof and the same is ordered to be certified.

| | |
|---|---|
| Ebenezer Rees | Plaintiff |
| vs | In Case |
| Arthur Cobb | Defendant |

By consent of the parties ordered this Suit be cont$^d$ till tomorrow.

| | | |
|---|---|---|
| Dun | Executors William Gilbert | Pltffs |
| | vs | In Case |
| Wal | Job & Richard Kories | Defendant |

This day came the Defendant by his atto and the plaintiff having been solemnly called came not but made default nor is his Suit further prosecuted therefore it is cons$^d$ by the Court that the Plaintiff be non Suited and that Defendant go hence without day & recover of the Pltff his costs by him about his Defense in this behalf expended.

| | | |
|---|---|---|
| Dun | David Ferguson | Plaintiff |
| | vs | Case |
| Har | Julian Thomas | Defendant |

By consent of the parties ordered that this Suit be continued

| | | |
|---|---|---|
| | John Holland | Plaintiff |
| | vs | in Case |
| | Elias Fisher | Defendant |

By consent ordered that this Suit be Continued

| | | |
|---|---|---|
| Mahan | John Jones | Plaintiff |
| | vs | Attachment |
| | Benjamine Thyre | |

This day came the plaintiff by his attorney and the Defendant being solemnly called & Still failing to appear and plead to Issue it is ordered that the office Judgment herein be confirmed & made final on motion to quash the Att$^o$ ordered that the Same be dismissed.

| | | |
|---|---|---|
| Dun | George Rapalie | Plaintiff |
| | vs | |
| Wal | John E. Long | Defendant |

The parties by their attorneys agree that this Suit be continued the plaintiff paying the costs thereof.

---

190

| | | |
|---|---|---|
| Har | W$^m$ Dunbar | Plaintiff |
| | vs | In Case |
| Duncan | Andrew Beal | Defendant |

Ordered that a Citation Issue against the Executers of the Deceased to come forward and Defend the Suit

| | | |
|---|---|---|
| Dun | William Vousdan | Plaintiff |
| | vs | Tresspass |
| Bra | Ex$^{tors}$ of Morris Stackpoole Dec$^d$. | Defendant |

The death of the plaintiff Suggested and David Ker and George Fitzgerald Executors of the last will and Testament of the S$^d$ Deceased enter their appearance to this Suit.

| | | |
|---|---|---|
| Ker | Lewis Valcourt | Plaintiff |
| | Vs | In Case |
| | Acres & McBride | Defendant |

This day came the plaintiff by his atto and the Defendant being Solemnly called doth not come nor Say anthing in bar or preclusion of the Plaintiff's action ags$^t$ him but hath made default whereby the Said Lewis Valcourt remains against them the Said Acres & McBride therein altogether undefended & because it is not known what Damages the plaintiff hath Sustained in the Promises it is ordered that the Same be enquired of and assessed by a Jury at the next court.

Ordered that Court be adj$^d$ till tomorrow morning 9 o'clock.

Court agreeable to adjournment Met
         Present
          Sam^l Brook &
          John Henderson Esqs

Ordered that court be adjourned till to morrow morning for want of a Sufficient Quorum.

       Court Met according to adj^t Saturday 10th 1803
         Present
          Samuel Brooks
          John Henderson Esqs
          & James Ferrall

Ordered that court be adjourned till Court in Course
         Sam^l Brooks J. P.
        Court

At a court held for the County of Adams at the Courthouse thereof in the City of Natchez on Monday the Sixth Day of March in the Year of Our Lord one thousand eight hundred and four
         Present
          Samuel Brooks
          John Henderson
          John Callender & Esquires
          James Ferrall

---

  William B. Shields Exhibited in Court a Licence from Cato West Secretary of the Territory Authorizing him to practice as an attorney and Counsellor at Law whereupon he took the oath Presented by Law and is admitted accordingly.

| | | |
|---|---|---|
|Har| Ebenezer Rees | Plaintiff |
| | Vs | in Case |
| | Arthur Cobb | Defendant |

This day came the plaintiff by their attos and /six words illegible, crossed out/ thereupon came a Jury to wit, Abram Guice, James West, Parson Carter, Reubin Gibson, John Congill, Nicholas Rabb, Abram Taylor, David Havard, Israel Leonard, John Mitchell, Thomas Ford & William Montgomery, who being elected tried & Sworn well and truly to try the Issue Joined upon their oath do say that the Defendant did assume upon himself in Manner and form as the Plaintiff against him hath declared and do assess the plaintiff damages by reason thereof to one hundred and Sixty Six Dollars and fifty cents besides Costs therefore it is considered by the Court that the Plaintiff recover against the Said Defendant his Damages aforesaid assessed also his costs by him about his suit in that behalf expended and the Defendant in Mercy &c

  Ordered that no attorney of this Court in any Cause Shall become Special Bail for any parties /one word illegible/ with the Special leave of the Court.

Peter Rabb Nathaniel Harrison & William Montgomery being Summonsed
to attend this Court this day as Jury men, were Solemnly called but came not
therefore it is Considered by the Court for their Contempt there in that
they be severally fined Six Dollars each to be applied for such default unless they appear and make a reasonable excuse as the Law directs & that they
may be taken &c whereupon the Said William Montgomery came into court and
made his excuse therefore his fine is remitted him.

Willi    Christopher Lee              Plaintiff
              vs                         in Case
Har    Miguel Sollivellas            Defendant

Ordered that the former rule of referance made herein be continued.
     Ordered that court be adjourned till half past two o'clock.
                          Court Met according to adjmt
                              Present
                                 Samuel Brooks
                                 Adam Tooley      Esqs
                                 James Ferrall
                                 Wm Darby

On the application of Captain Israel Luce who produced in court a certificate
of his fitness to keep a Tavern at his house in the County it is ordered that
a Licence be granted him to keep the Said Tavern during the term of one year
from the date hereof and until the next succeeding Court thereafter he having
entered into & acknowledged bond in the Sum of three hundred with Jas Cole
& Morris Custard his Trustee Con't according to Law.

---

    William Kenner              Plaintiff
         vs                         On a Scire facias vs Bail
    Morris Custard Bail of       Defendant
       Elias Fisher

In this case Morris Custard brought into court the body of the Said Elias
Fisher and Surrend him in discharge of his bail & the Said Morris is exon
orated on Paying the Costs of this suit.

    Daniel Douglass             Plaintiff
         vs                         Case
    Henry Green                  Defendant

This day came the Defendant by his by his Attorney and the Plaintiff having
been Solemnly called came not therefore it is considered by the court that
the Plaintiff be non Suited and that he go henence without Day and recover
of the Plaintiff his costs by him about his Suit in that behalf expended
Whereupon the Said Plaintiff by his attorney comes into Court and on Motion
of the Sd Plaintiff it is ordered that the order made herein be Set aside
and the cause be continued.

---

Pain     Ferdinand L. Claiborne      Plaintiff
Recorded    Vs                         In Debt
         Leonard B. Compton         Defendant

This day came the Plaintiff by his attorney and the Defendant in Proper Person and the Said Defendant acknowledges the plaintiff's action, therefore it is considered by the Court that the Plaintiff recover against the Said Defendant the Sum of two hundred and Seventy one Dollars and Sixty two Cents the Debt in the Decln Mentioned with Intrest thereon besides Costs &c the Pltff agrees to stay the Execution of this Judgment till the first Day of January 1805 and the Said Defendant in Mercy &c

Pain Recorded

|  |  |  |
|---|---|---|
| Same | | Plaintiff |
| vs | | In Case |
| Same | | Defendant |

This day came the Plaintiff by his attorney and the Defendant in Proper person and the Said Defendant acknowledges the Plaintiff's action therefore it is considered by the Court that the Plaintiff recover against the Said Defendant thirty two Dollars with Intrest thereon besides Costs, and the Plaintiff agrees to stay the Execution of this Judgment till the first day of January 1805 and the Said Defendant in Mercy &c

Wal

|  |  |
|---|---|
| Francis Killer | Plaintiff |
| vs | In Case |
| Andrew McBride | Defendant |

This day John Hoggatt as Special Bail delivered up the body of the Defendant in Discharge of his recognizance & undertaking & the Defendant prayed in Custody &c.

|  |  |
|---|---|
| Manuel Lopez | Plaintiff |
| vs | on a Scire facias against bail |
| Anthony Dougherty & | Defendant |
| Patrick Connally bail of | |
| Christopher Lee | |

In this case Anthony Dougherty and Patrick Connally brought into court the body of the Said Christopher Lee and Surrendered him in discharge of their bail & the Said Anthony Dougherty & Patrick Connally are exonerated in paying the Costs of this suit.

Wal

|  |  |
|---|---|
| Daniel Douglass | Plaintiff |
| Vs | In Debt |
| Charles Dowling | Defendant |

Wal

|  |  |
|---|---|
| Same | Plaintiff |
| Vs | In Case |
| Same 2nd Suit | Defendant |
| Same | Plaintiff |
| vs | Same |
| Same 3rd Suit | Defendant |

John Parker the Defendants Spl Bl in the above suits Deld up the body of the Said Deft in Discharge of his Recgns & undertaking & the Deft in Custody &c

Certified   Daniel Hawley Presented in Court an Acct agst the County which being examined is allowed and ordered to be certified for forty three Dollars and twenty-nine cents.   $43 29

Ordered that court be adjourned till tomorrow morning nine o'clock.
Tuesday 7th 1804, Court met acording to adjournment met

Present
Samuel Brooks
Adam Toolley
William Foster &
William Darby
} Esquires

| | | |
|---|---|---|
| Dp | John Croker | Plaintiff |
| Recorded | vs | in Case |
| Wal | Martin Hinderlider | Defendant |

This day came the parties by their attornies and thereupon came a Jury to wit Abram Guice, James West, Parson Carter, Reubin Gibson, John Cowgill, Nicholas Rabb, Abram Taylor, David Havard, Israel Leonard, John Mitchell, Thomas Ford & William Montgomery, who being Elected tried and Sworn well and truly to try the Issue Joined upon their Oath do say that the Defendant did not undertake & promise in manner and form as the Plaintiff in his Declaration against him hath declared therefore it is considered by the Court that the Defendant go hence without day & recover of Pltff his Costs &c

---

198

James Wilson  Plaintiff
vs  Case
Benjamine Kitchens  Defendant

Ordered that the former Rule of Reference in this cause be discharged & continued.

John Willson  Plaintiff
vs  in Case
Lewis Evans  Defendant

James Wallace administrator of the Said John Willson comes into court and appears to the Suit & continues for trial at the next term.

| | | |
|---|---|---|
| Har | David Ferguson & Melling Woolley, | Plaintiffs |
| | vs | Case |
| Wal | Patrick Connally | Defendant |

Ordered by consent of the parties that the former Rule of Reference be continued if no award be returned in this cause within Six weeks then the Said Award to be set aside & set for trial at the next term.

| | | |
|---|---|---|
| Frank | George Rapalie | Plaintiff |
| Recorded | vs | In Case |
| Wal | John E. Long | Defendant |

This day came the Defendant by his attorney and the plaintiff being Solemnly called came not therefore it is considered by the Court that the Plaintiff be non Suited and the Defendant go hence without day and recover of the Pltff his costs by him about his defense in that behalf expended

Thomas Wilkins          Plaintiff
    vs                  In Case
Stephen Stephenson      Defendant
by consent of the Parties ordered this Suit be continued.

Thomas Regan            Plaintiff
    vs                  in Case
Benjamine Kitchens      Defendant
Ordered that the former Rule of Reference in the cause be Set aside.

W$^m$ McWilliams        Plaintiff
    Vs                  in Case
The Same                Defendant
Ordered that the former Rule of reference in this Cause be Set aside.

William Dunbar          Plaintiff
    Vs                  Case
Andrew Beall            Defendant
Ordered that a Citation issue to Rich$^d$ Beall Executor of the Last Will and Testament of the Said Andrew Beall deceased to come forward & Defend Suit.

---

Ferguson & Woolley      Plaintiff
    vs
Andrew Beall            Defendant
Ordered that a citation Issue against Rich$^d$ Beall Executor of the Last Will and Testament of Andrew Beall deceased to come forward & defend this suit.

A. Hunt                 Plaintiff
    vs                  in Case
Peter Anthony           Defendant
By consent ordered this suit be Continued.

Dun         Stephen Adair       Plaintiff
Recorded        vs              in Case
Marny       Nancy Martin        Defendant
This day came the Defendant by her attorney & the plaintiff being Solemnly called came not therefore it is Considered by the court that the plaintiff be non Suited and that the Defendant go hence without Day and recover of the Plaintiff her Costs by about her Defence on that behalf expended.

Ordered that Court be adj$^d$ till tomorrow morning 9 o'clock.

---

Court Met agreeable to adjournment
    Present
        Samuel Brooks
        A. Tooley
        W$^m$ Darby     Esquires
        W$^m$ Foster
        James Ferrall
        Jacob Guise
        John Henderson
        John Callender

| | | |
|---|---|---|
| Har | Henry Churchill | Plaintiff |
| Recorded | vs | in Case |
| Tur | Moses Moore | Defendant |

This day came the parties by their attornies and the Said Defendant by his attorney relinquishing his former Plea and Saving and reserving to himself every advantage he may have in Equity. Says he cannot gainsay the Plaintiff's action against him Therefore it is considered by the court that the Plaintiff recover against the Said Defendant one hundred and thirty Six Dollars and fifty Cents & also his costs by him about his Suit in that behalf expended & the Said Defendant in Mercy &c

---

202

It is considered by the Court that they have not now a right to levy a Tax on the County for the Purpose of building a Jail & Courthouse agreeable to an act of Assembly Passed 18th of November 1803 entitled an act to establish a permanant Site of Justice for the District County of Adams.

| | | |
|---|---|---|
| Wal | James Wiley | Plaintiff |
| Recorded | vs | In case |
| | Lewis Evans | Defendant |

This day came the Plaintiff by his attorneys and the Defendant in Proper Person and the Said Defendant acknowledges the plaintiffs action therefore it is considered by the Court that the plaintiff recover against the Said Defendant the sum of twelve Dollars besides his costs by him about his suit in that behalf expended and the Said Defendant in Mercy &c

| | | |
|---|---|---|
| Ex^tors | Morris Stackpoole | Plaintiff |
| | vs | Case |
| | W^m B. Smith | Defendant |

Refered by consent to Love Baker and his award to be made the Judgment of the Court & Execution to Issue thereon

                                        Absent
                                            John Callender
                                            William Darby   Esquires
                                            James Ferrell &
                                            Samuel Brooks

---

203

| | | |
|---|---|---|
| Wal | Patrick Connelly | Plaintiff |
| Recorded | vs | In Trover |
| Mahan | Thomas Crabb | Defendant |

This day came the Defendant by his attorney & the Plaintiff being Solomnly called came not therefore it is therefore considered by the Court that the Plaintiff be non Suited and that the Defendant go hence without Day and recover of the Said Plaintiff his costs by him about his Suit in that behalf expended.

| | | |
|---|---|---|
| | William Dunbar | Plaintiff |
| | vs | Case |
| | Jeremiah Bass | Defendant |

Referred to John Henderson Esq^r his award to be returned and made the Judgment of the court.

Joseph Martinez             Plaintiff
    vs
David Kennady               Defendant

Ordered that a Citation Issue to Jesse Withers Adm$^r$ of the Said Deed.
Ordered that Court be adjurned till 2 o'clock.

204

Court Met at 2 o'clock agreeable to adjournment.
                Present
                    Samuel Brooks
                    John Henderson
                    Adam Toolley       Esquires
                    Alexander Montgomery
                        &
                    W$^m$ Foster

Stephen Terry               Plaintiff
    vs
John Lusk                   Defendant

By consent ordered this Suit be continued.

A Deed of Bargain & Sale from Joseph W. A. Loyd to the Commissioners appointed by an act of assembly for the purpose of establishing a Site of Justice for the District and County of Adams was presented in Court acknowledged by the Said Joseph and ordered to be recorded.

             Alexander Farrar          Plaintiff
Recorded        Vs                     Case
             Ebenezer Rees             Defendant

This day came the parties by their attornies and the Deft. by his attorney relinquishing his former Plea acknowledges the plaintiffs action therefore it is considered by the Court that the Plaintiff recover against the Defendant the sum of seventy Seven Dollars and eighty one cents also his costs by him about his Suit in that behalf expended &c with Stay of execution till next term.

[Pages 205 and 206 missing]

207

Har       James Lewis Cast            Plaintiff
Recorded      Vs                      Trover
          Babptest Monela             Defendant

This day came the Plaintiff by his Attorney and thereupon came a Jury to wit, the same Jury as first aforesaid, who being elected tried and Sworn well and truly to enquire of damages in this suit Ret$^d$ Verdict "we the Jury find for the Plaintiff one Cent Damage besides costs. Therefore it is considered by the Court that the Plaintiff recover against the said Defendant his Dam: aforesaid in manner and form by the Jurors in their verdict aforesaid assessed also his costs by him about his suit in this behalf expended and the said Deft in Mercy &$^c$.

| | | |
|---|---|---|
| Har | John Walton | Plaintiff |
| Recorded | vs | In Case |
| | Robert Wilson | Defendant |

This day came the Plaintiff by his Attorney and thereupon came a Jury to wit, the Same Jury as first aforesaid, who being elected tried and Sworn well and truly to enquire of Damages in this Suit Returned Verdict "We of the Jury find for the Plaintiff eighty nine Dollars in Damages besides Costs". therefore it is considered by the Court that the plaintiff recover against the Said Deft his Damages aforesaid in Manner and form by the Jurors in their verdict aforesaid assessed also his costs by him about his suit in this behalf expended & The Defendant in Mercy &c

---

| | | |
|---|---|---|
| Har | Walker & Henderson | Plaintiff |
| Recorded | vs | in Case |
| | Little Berry West | Defendant |

This Day came the Plaintiff by his attorney and thereupon came a Jury to wit, the Same Jury as first aforesaid, who being elected tried and Sworn Well and truly to enquire of Damages in this suit Returned verdict "We the Jury find for the plaintiff fifty Seven Dollars and Seven cents Damages besides Costs" Therefore it is considered by the Court that the Plaintiff recover against the Defendant his Damages aforesaid in Manner and form by the Jurors in their verdict aforesaid assessed also his Costs by him about his Suit in that behalf expended and the Said Defendant in Mercy &c

| | | |
|---|---|---|
| Har | St James Beauvais & Co. | Plaintiff |
| Recorded | vs | In Case |
| | George Lawnig | Defendant |

This day came the Plaintiff by his attorney and thereupon came a Jury to wit, the Same Jury as on the Suit Thomas Erwin against Charles Cayson, who being elected tried and Sworn well and truly to enquire of Damages in this Suit Returned Verdict "We of the Jury find for the Plaintiff ninety Seven Dollars and Eighty five cents Damages besides cost. Therefore it is considered by the court that the Plaintiff recover against the Said Defendant his damages aforesaid in Manner and form by the Jurors in their verdict aforesaid assessed also his costs by him about his Suit in this behalf expended and the Said Defendant in Mercy &c

---

| | | |
|---|---|---|
| Har | Lewis Valcourt | Plaintiff |
| Recorded | vs | In Case |
| | Acres & McBride | Defendant |

This day came the Plaintiff by his attorney and thereupon came a Jury as on the Suit Erwin against Cayson Who being elected tried and Sworn well and truly to enquire of Damages in this Suit Returned Verdict "We the Jury find for the Plaintiff Seventy two Dollars and forty five cents Damages besides Costs" therefore it is considered by the Court that the Plaintiff recover against the said Defendant his Damages aforesaid in Manner and form by the Jurors in their Verdict aforesaid assessed also his Costs by him about his Suit in that behalf expended and the Defendant in Mercy &c

| | | |
|---|---|---|
| Duncan | Robert Moore | Plaintiff |
| Recorded | vs | in Case |
| | John Tally | Defendant |

This day came the Plaintiff by his Attorneys and thereupon came a Jury to wit the Same Jury as on the Suit Erwin against Cayson who being elected tried and Sworn well & truly to enquire of Damages in this Suit Returned verdict "We the Jury find for the Plaintiff eighty one Dollars and fifty Six Cents Damages & Costs" therefore it is considered by the Court that the plaintiff recover against the Defendant his Damages aforesaid in Manner and form by the Jurors in their Verdict aforesaid assessed also his costs by him about his suit in that behalf expended and the Deft in Mercy &c

| | | |
|---|---|---|
| Wal | George Darby | Plaintiff |
| Recorded | vs | in Case |
| | William Bragg | Defendant |

This day came the Plaintiff by his attorney and thereupon came also a Jury to wit, the Same Jury as on the Suit Evans vs Cayson, who being elected tried and Sworn well & truly to enquire of Damages in his Suit Returned Verdict "We the Jury find for the Plaintiff one cent Damage and costs of Suit" therefore it is considered by the Court that the Plaintiff recover against the Defendant his Damages aforesaid in manner and form by the Jurors in their Verdict aforesaid assessed also his costs by him about his Suit in this behalf expended and the Said Defendant in Mercy &c

| | | |
|---|---|---|
| Wal | Joseph Singleton | Plaintiff |
| Recorded | vs | in Case |
| | John Replie | Defendant |

This day came the Plaintiff by his attorney and thereupon came also a Jury to wit, The same Jury as on the Suit Erwin against Cayson who being elected tried and Sworn well and truly to enquire of Damages in this suit Returned Verdict "We of the Jury find for the Plaintiff one cent Damages and costs of suit" Therefore it is considered by the Court that the Plaintiff recover against the Defendant his Damages aforesaid in Manner and form by the Jurors in their Verdict aforesaid assessed also his costs by him about his Suit in that behalf expended and the Said Defendant in Mercy &c

| | |
|---|---|
| Ebenezer Rees | Plaintiff |
| Vs | in Case |
| Lewis Duvell | Defendant |

This day came the Plaintiff by his Attorney and and thereupon came also a Jury to wit, the Same Jury as on the Suit Erwin against Cayson, who being elected tried and Sworn well and truly to enquire of Damages in this Suit Returned Verdict "We of the Plaintiff thirty Eight Dollars thirty Seven and one half cents in Damages besides costs" therefore it is considered by the Court that the Plaintiff recover against the Defendant his Damages aforesaid in Manner and form by the Jurors on this Verdict aforesaid assessed also his costs by him about his suit in this behalf expended and the Said Defendant in Mercy &c

Frances Nailor          Plaintiff
vs          in Case
Stephen Stephenson          Defendant

Charles Kin appearance bail Surrendered up the body of the Defendant in Discharge of recognizance and undertaking and said Defendant prays in Custody & whereupon Samuel Timberlake comes into Court and undertakes for the Said Deft that in case he shall be cast in the Suit aforesaid That he would Satisfy and pay the Costs and condemnation of the Court or surrender his body in execution for the Same or in case of failure thereof that he the Said Samuel Timberlake would do it for him.

---

Ordered that Samuel Brooks and John Henderson Esquires be continued as Commissioners to lay off the Boundaries for the Jail and that they be authorized to alter the Present Boundery and fix them the most convenient to the present prison that they Shall Judgement and that the bounds be established upon their report into office.

Solomon Swayze          Plaintiff
vs          Attachment
Elijah Cockefair          Defendant

Ordered by the Court that the Property attached be sold by the Sheriff and the money arising from Such Sale be deposited as the Law directs.

Ordered that the Court be adjourned till tomorrow morning 9 o'clock.

---

Court Met according to adjournment
    Present
      Adam Toolley
      John Henderson
      William Foster    Esquires
      Jacob Guice

Recorded      United States          Plaintiff
            vs          in Debt
            David Johnson & Hogg          Defendant

This day came the U. S. by its Attorney and the Defendant in Proper Person and the Said Defendant acknowledges the Said action of the United States, therefore it is considered by the Court that the Said United States recover against the Defendant the Sum of ninety nine Dollars fifty one and three fourth cents the Debt in the Declaration mentioned with legal interest thereon till Paid also the Costs about the Same Suit in that behalf expended and the Said Defendant in Mercy &$^c$. Stay Ex$^{on}$ 15$^{th}$ May.

Same      Same          Plaintiff
        vs          In Debt
        Same          Defendant

This day came the U. S. by its atto. and the Deft in Proper person and the Said Deft acknowledges the 3$^d$ action of the Said U. S. therefore it is

Considered by the Court that the S$^d$ U. S. recover against the Said Defendants the Sum of ninety nine Dollars fifty one and three fourths cents the Debt in the Declaration mentioned with legal interest thereon till paid also the costs about the Same Suit in that behalf expended and the Deft in Mercy &c Stay execution 15$^{th}$ May.

214

|  | John W. Langford | Plaintiff |
|---|---|---|
| Recorded | Vs | in Case |
| Wal | Joseph Griffin | Defendant |

This day came the Defendant by his attorney and the Plaintiff being Solemnly called came not therefore it is considered by the Court that the plaintiff be non Suited and that the Defendant go hence without Day and recover of the Plaintiff his Costs by him about his defence in this behalf expended.

| Wal | Ann Martin | Plaintiff |
|---|---|---|
| Recorded | vs | in Case |
| Dun | Ebenezer Reese | Defendant |

This day came the Parties by their attornies and thereupon came a Jury to wit Abram Guice, James West Parson Carter Reubin Gibson, John Cowgill, Nicholas Rabb David Havard Israel Leonard William Montgomory, Thomas Ford, William B. Smith Jun$^r$ & John E. Long, who being elected tried and Sworn well and truly to try the Issue Joined and the plaintiff being Solemnly called came not and the Jury from rendering their verdict are discharged, nor is her Suit further Prosecuted therefore it is considered by the Court that the Plaintiff be non suited and that the Defendant go hence without day and recover of the Plaintiff his Costs by her about his Suit in that behalf expended.

215

| Certified | Anthony Dougherty Exhibited in Court an account against the County which being examined is allowed and ordered to be Certified for forty four Dollars & fifty cents | $44.50 Cents. |
|---|---|---|
| Wal | Sarah Dunnavans | Plaintiff |
| Recorded | Vs | Tresspass |
| Dun | Moses Caroll | Defendant |

This day came the Parties by their attornies and thereupon came a Jury to wit, Abram Guice James West, Prosper Carter, Reubin Gibson, John Cowgill, Nicholas Rabb, David Havard, Israel Leonard, William Montgomery, Thomas Ford W$^m$ B. Smith Jun$^r$ & John Mitchell who being elected tried and Sworn well and truly to try the Issue Joined upon their oath do say that the Defendant is guilty in Manner and form as the plaintiff against him in her Declaration hath declared and do assess the plaintiff Damages by reason thereof to three hundred and eighty nine dollars and twenty five cents Damages besides Costs therefore it is considered by the Court that the Plaintiff recover against the Defendant her Damages aforesaid in Manner and form by the Jurors in their verdict aforesaid assessed also her costs by him about her suit in that behalf expended and the Said Defendant in Mercy &c.

|  |  |  |
|---|---|---|
| Har | Jerry Brandon | Plaintiff |
|  | Vs | attachment |
|  | Roderick & Robert Perry | Defts |

William Lemon Garnishee answereth on oath that he Stands Indebted to Robert Perry one of the Defendants in the Sum of four hundred dollars for a Negro boy for which sum the Said Robert hold this Garnishee obligation Payable the fourteenth of February last and that he hath no other effects of the Defendants or either of them in his hands

Present
Alex$^r$ Montgomery Esq$^r$

Ordered on Motion of John E. Long that a Tavern Licence be granted him to keep a Tavern at his house in this County during the term of one year from the date hereof and until the next Succeeding Court thereafter he having Complained [one word illegible crossed out] and entered into & acknowledged Bond with F. L. Claiborne & W$^m$ Brooks his Surities in the Sum of three hundred Dollars conditioned according to law.

Ordered that Court adjourned till 2 o'clock.

Court met according to adjournment
Present
John Henderson
W$^m$ Foster  Esquires
Jonathan Guice
Alexander Montgomery

---

|  |  |  |
|---|---|---|
| Har | Ferguson & Woolley | Plaintiff |
| Recorded | vs | case |
| May | Joptha Higdon | Defendant |

This day came the Parties by their attornies and the Said Parties agree to Waved the trial of the Issue by a Jury and agree to put themselves on the Judgment of the Court and being fully heard it is the opinion of the Court that the Defendant did assume in Manner and form as the plaintiff in his Declaration hath alledged and do assess the plaintiff Damages by reason thereof to Seventy Seven Dollars and fifty five Cents besides cost therefore it is considered by the court that the plaintiff against the Said Defendant his Damages aforesaid in Manner & form aforesaid given also his Costs by him about his Suit in this behalf expended & the Defendant in Mercy &c

Ordered that David Greenleaf, John Martin, William Montgomery Daniel Fowler, Benjamine Newman, Archibald Lewis & Samuel Montgomery do view & mark out a Road on the South fork of Cole's Creek Beginning near John Martin's running thro Captain Greenleaf's and a part of Captain Morrow's District untill it intersects the public highway near Daniel Whitaker's and make report thereof according to law.

---

|  |  |
|---|---|
| Silas L. Pain | Plaintiff |
| vs |  |
| Joptha Higdon | Defendant |

Death of the plaintiff suggested.

(218-220)

|     | Peter A. Vandorn | Plaintiff |
|-----|------------------|-----------|
|     | vs               | Case      |
|     | Silas L. Pain    | Defendant |

Death of the Defendant suggested

| Wal | Nathaniel Tomlinson | Plaintiff |
|-----|---------------------|-----------|
|     | vs                  | Case      |
| Dp  | Seth Caston         | Defendant |

Ordered that the former rule of Reference in this cause be set aside.
Ordered that Court be adjourned till tomorrow morning 9 o'clock.

---

219

Court agreeable to adjournment met
Present
Alex$^{or}$ Montgomery
Adam Toolley     Esquires
W$^m$ Foster &
Samuel Boyd

On the application of Ferdinand L. Claborne it is ordered by the Court that William Darby Esquire be appointed as Enquirer in his Room and Stead to take & Receive a list of the Taxable Property in the District for which the Said F. L. Claiborne is appointed for the Current year.

| Thomas Berry | Plaintiff |
|--------------|-----------|
| Vs           | in Case   |
| John Shute   | Defendant |

This day came the Defendant by his and the Plaintiff being Solemnly called came not therefore it is considered by the Court that the Plaintiff be non Suited and that the Deft go hence without day and recover against the Plaintiff his costs by him about his defence in that behalf expended.

---

220

| Har | William Thompson | Plaintiff |
|-----|------------------|-----------|
| Recorded | vs | In Trover |
| Mahan | Rowland Shackleford | Defendant |

This day came the Parties by their attornies and thereupon came a Jury To Wit, Abram Guice, James West, Parson Carter, Reubin Gibson, John Cowgill, Nicholas Rabb, Daniel Havard, Isreal Leonard, Anthony Calvit, Thomas Ford, John Mitchell, David Gibson who being elected tried and Sworn well and truly to try the Issue Joined upon their oath do say that the Defendant is guilty in Manner and form as the plaintiff in his Declaration hath alledged and do assess the plaintiff damages By reason thereof to Twenty five Dollars besides Costs therefore it is considered by the Court that the Plaintiff recover against the Said Deft his damages aforesaid in Manner and form by the Jurors in their verdict aforesaid assessed and also his Costs by him about his Suit in that behalf expended and the Said Defendant in Mercy &c

|          | John Overaker for use of Drake, | Plaintiff |
|----------|-------------------------------|-----------|
| Recorded | vs                            | in Case   |
|          | James Ferrall                 | Defendant |

This day came the parties by their attornies and thereupon came a Jury The Same Jury as next above who being elected tried and sworn the truth to Speak upon the Issue, Joined upon their oath do say that the Defendant hath not Paid the Debt in the Decl aforesaid mentioned as in pleading he hath alledged as do assess the Plaintiff Damages by reason thereof to thirty one Dollars and twenty five cents besides Costs therefore it is considered by the Court that the Plaintiff recover against the Defendant his Damages aforesaid in Manner and form by the Jurors in their verdict aforesaid assessed and also his costs by him about his Suit in that behalf expended and the Deft in Mercy &c

Ordered that court be adjourned till 2 o'clock.
Court Met according to adjournment
Present
Samuel Brooks
William Foster
S. Boyd &
A. Montgomery
Esquires

Jeremiah Ruth — Plaintiff
vs
Moses Ousteen — Defendant

This day came the Defendant by his attorney and the Plaintiff being Solemnly called came not therefore it is considered by the Court that the plaintiff be non suited and that the Defendant go hence without day and recover agst the plaintiff his costs by him about his defence in that behalf expended and thereupon the Said Plaintiff comes into court and moved the Court that his cause be reinstated which is granted him & it is ordered that Commissions Issue to take the depositions of absent witnesses on Interrogations.

Hoggatt et als — Plaintiff
vs — in Case
Barton Hannon — Defendant

This day came the Parties by their attornies and thereupon came a Jury To wit Abram Guice, James West, Parson Carter, Reubin Gibson, John Cowgill, Nicholas Rabb, David Havard, Israel Leonard, Thomas Ford, John Mitchell, David Gibson, Thomas Hieth, who being elected tried & Sworn well and truly to try the Issue Joined upon their oath do say that the

Defendant did promise and undertake in Manner and form as stated in the Plaintiff's declaration and do assess the Pltff Damages by reason thereof to one hundred & fifty one Dollars and fifty one cents Damages besides costs, therefore it is considered by the court that the Plaintiff recover against the Said Defendant his Damages aforesaid assessed also his Costs by him about his Suit in that behalf expended and the Said Deft in Mercy &c

Har   A. Hunt — Plaintiff
Recorded  vs — In /Blank/
Tur   John Blanchard — Defendant

This day came the Parties by their attornies and thereupon came a Jury to wit Abram Guice, James West, Parson Carter, Reubin Gibson, John Cowgill, Nicholas Rabb, David Havard, Israel Leonard, Thomas Ford, David Mitchell,

(222-224)

David Gibson, Thomas Heith who being elected tried and sworn well and truly to try the Issue Joined upon their Oath do say that the Defendant did Promise and undertake in manner & form as the Plaintiff in his Declaration hath alle$^d$-ged and do assess the Damages by reason thereof to Sixty Seven Dollars besides Costs, therefore it is considered by the Court that the Plaintiff recover against the Said Defendant his Damages aforesaid in Manner and form by the Jurors in their verdict aforesaid assessed also his Costs by him about his suit in that behalf expended and the Def$^t$ in Mercy &$^c$

|          | Richard Down | Plaintiff |
|----------|--------------|-----------|
| Recorded | Vs           |           |
|          | Joseph Lee   | Def$^t$   |

This day came &$^c$ the Same Jury as next above Returned Verdict for the Plaintiff for forty three Dollars Damages & Costs.

---

223

|       | James Ferrall   | Plaintiff |
|-------|-----------------|-----------|
| Har   |                 |           |
| Lewis | Vs              | In Case   |
| Ex$^{on}$ for costs | William Henery | Defendant |

This day came the parties by their attorneys and thereupon came a Jury to wit Abram Guice, James West, Parson Carter, Reubin Gibson, John Cowgill, Nicholas Rabb, David Havard, Israel Leonard, Thomas Ford, John Mitchell, David Gibson Thomas Hieth, who being elected tried and Sworn well and truly to try the Issue Joined upon their oath do say that the Defendant did assume on himself in manner and form as the plaintiff his Declaration hath alledged and do assess the plaintiff Damages by Occasion thereof to three hundred dollars besides costs, therefore it is considered by the court that the Plaintiff recover against the Defendant his Damages aforesaid in manner and form by the Jurors in their verdict aforesaid assessed also his costs by him about his Suit in that behalf expended and the said Defendant in Mercy &$^c$

|          | The Same | Plaintiff |
|----------|----------|-----------|
| Har      |          |           |
| Recorded | vs       | in Case   |
| Lewis    | The Same | Defendant |

This day came the Parties by their attorneys and thereupon came a Jury to wit Abram Guice, James West, Parson Carter, Reubin Gibson, John Cowgill, Nicholas Robb, David Havard, Israel Leonard, Thomas Ford, John Mitchell, David Gibson & Thomas Hieth, who being elected tried and sworn well and truly to try the Issue Joined upon their oath do say that the Deft did undertake and promise in manner and form as the Pltff

---

224

in his Declaration hath declared and do assess the Plaintiff Damages by occasion thereof to fifty eight Dollars twelve and one half cents besides Costs therefore it is considered by the court that the plaintiff recover against the Defendant his Damages aforesaid in manner and form by the Jurors in their verdict aforesaid assessed also his costs by him about his suit in that behalf & the Said Defendant in Mercy &$^c$

| | |
|---|---|
| Same | Plaintiff |
| vs | in Debt |
| Same & John Henry | Defendant |

This day came the Parties by their attornies and thereupon came a Jury to wit Abram Guice, James West, Parson Carter, Roubin Gibson, John Cowgill, Nicholas Rabb, David Havard, Israel Leonard, Thomas Ford, John Mitchell, David Gibson & Thomas Hieth who being elected tried and sworn well and truly to try the Issue Joined upon their oath do say that the Def$^{td}$ did undertake & Promise in manner & form as the Plaintiff agst him hath declared and find for the Plaintiff forty three Dollars twelve and one half cents, the Debt in the Decl mentioned also one cent Damages besides Costs therefore it is considered by the court that the plaintiff recover against the Defendant his Debts Damages & Costs aforesaid in Manner and form by the Jurors in their verdict aforesaid assessed also his costs by him about his Suit in that behalf.

| | |
|---|---|
| Charles McBride Adm$^r$ | Plaintiff |
| vs | in Case |
| Alexander Montgomery | Defendant |

By consent commission is awarded the Defendant to take the Deposition of Henry Bowger being listed or giving the Pltff notice of the time & place to buy.

Court adj$^d$ till tomorrow 9 o'clock.

---

225

Court agreeable to adjournment met
Present
Sam$^l$ Brooks
Wm Foster
Sam$^l$ Boyd          Esquires
John Callender
William Darby

Every cause when called shall be immediatly tried Cont$^d$ or discontinued - No cause shall be continued unless by consent or on Sufficient cause shown by affidavit or otherwise to the satisfaction of the court - Jurors making Default shall be fined.

Ordered by the court
Signed
Sam$^l$ Brooks

| | |
|---|---|
| Benjamine Robinson | Plaintiff |
| vs | |
| Bennett Truly | Defendant |

by consent of the Parties it is ordered that either Party take depositions without the Territory before any legal Justice of the Peace or Alcaid or interrogatories filed or notice given of the adverse party of the time & place of taking same.

| | |
|---|---|
| Bennett Truly | Plaintiff |
| vs | |
| Benjamine Robinson | Defendant |

By consent of the Parties it is ordered that either party take depositions without the Territory before any legal Justice of the Peace or Alcaid or interrogatories, filed or notice given the adverse Party of the time and place of taking the same.

W^m Pope & Co.       Plaintiff
 vs           in Case
Philip B. & John Compton   Defendant

This day came the plaintiffs by their attorney and the Defendant in Proper Person and the Said Defendant acknowledges the Plaintiff's action therefore it is considered by the court that the Plaintiff recover against the Defendant the sum of five hundred and fifty five Dollars Seventy two cents Interest and costs of a former Judgment with Interest on this Judgment till Paid & costs by him about their Present Suit in this behalf expended & the Defendant in Mercy &c

 Ordered that Court be adjourned till 2 o'clock.

        Court agreeable to adjournment met
          Present
          William Darby
          W^m Foster    Esquires
          Sam^l Boyd

Barnaba Minyard      Plaintiff
 vs           in /Blank/
Archibald Evans       Defendant

This day came the Defendant by his attorney and the Plaintiff failing to file his declaration agreeable to the rules of this court and being Solemnly called came not therefore it is ordered by the court that the Plaintiff be non Suited and that the Defendant go hence without Day and recover of the Plaintiff his costs by him about his defence in that behalf expended &c

---

 Charles B. Green produced in court a Licence from Cato West Secretary of the territory Authorising him to Practice as an attorney & Counsellor at Law Whereupon he took the usual Oath of office and is admitted accordingly.

Reed & Ford       Plaintiff
 vs           Case
Ezekiel Dewitt       Defendant

On motion of the Plaintiff leave is granted him to amend the first count of his declaration by inserting the name of William B. Smith instead of Ezekiel Dewitt and time given to plead there till the first of May.

 Ordered that Joshua Howard nominate such fit persons to whom the children of James Kelly may be bound as apprentices and return these persons so nominated to the next orphans court to the next Court for their approbation or rejection of the court.

Certified   Doct David Lattemore Exhib^t in Court an account ag^st the county after Examination is allowed and ordered to be certified for forty two Dollars and twenty five cents        42.25
 Benjamine Seamans the Same for   104.12

William Brenburg       Plaintiff
 vs
Joshua Hadley        Defendant

Ordered by consent of the parties that didimus Issue to take Despositions on interrogatories before any Justice of the Peace notice thereof being given to either party ten days

             William Darby J. P.

 Court adjourned till Court in Course.

At a County Court helf for the County of Adams at the Court House thereof in the City of Natchez on Monday the fourth Day of June 1804

Present
Samuel Brooks
John Henderson
Alexander Montgomery Esquires
James Neilson &
William Foster

Ferdinand L. Claiborn    Plaintiff
vs
John Bryan    Defendant

This day Joseph Harrison & John Bradshaw The Defendants Special Bail Surrendered up the body of the S$^d$ Defendant in discharge of their Recognizance and undertaking and the Said Defendant Prays in Custody &c

Ordered by the Court that a Permanent Bridge shall be built over the St Catherines where the main road leading from Natchez to Coles Creek crosses to, by Paid out of County Tax the court will receive Proposal till Tuesday the seventh Instant for building the same & the Clerk is ordered to put up at the Door of the Courthouse a notification thereof.

---

Lewis   Charles Norwood    Plaintiff
Recorded   Vs    in /Blank/
  Benj$^n$ Balk & Jeptha Higdon   Defendant

The plaintiff by his attorney comes into Court and says he will not prosecute this action further against the Defendant Jeptha Higdon and the Def$^t$ Benjimine Balk in Proper Person comes into court and acknowledges the Plaintiffs action for the sum of two hundred and eighty one Dollars and five cents damages besides Costs, therefore it is considered by the court that the Plaintiff recover against the Defendant the damages aforesaid & also his costs by him about his suit in that behalf expended and the Def$^t$ in mercy &c and the Plaintiff agrees to stay Exc$^n$ on this Judg$^t$ till first of Jan$^ry$

Paid my fees,
B. Seamans

The commissioners appointed to view & mark the roads on the South fork of Coles Creek this day returned their report which is as follows: agreeable to the order from the Worshipful Court of Adams County to us directed we have Proceeded to view and mark a Road from the neighourhood of John Martins to Daniel Whitakers and Pass there the land of David Greenleaf by consent, thence thro the lands of John Martin by consent, thence thro the land of Adam Bergamin, thence thro the land of Patrick Connelly, thence thro the lands of Benjamine Newman, by consent thence thro the lands of Charles Boardman lines thence thro the lands of James Carpenter and Daniel Whitaker by

consent Given under our hands this 27th Day of May 1804 and it is ordered by the Court that the same be established.

Har         James Ferrall              Plaintiff
Recorded         vs                    in Debt
            William Leland             Defendant

This day came the Plaintiff by his attorney and the Defendant in Proper Person and the Defendant acknowledges the plaintiffs action for the Debt in Declaration mentioned, of Eighty four Dollars eighty seven and one half cents with interest thereon for being Six Dollars & thirty six cents.

Specially & Costs therefore it is considered by the court that the plaintiff recover against the Said Defendant the Debt aforesaid with Interest as aforesaid also his costs by him about his Suit in that behalf expended & the Defendant be in Mercy &c the Pltff agree to Stay the Execution on this Judgment till the first Day of November next.

Dep         A. L. Duncan               Plaintiff
Recorded         Vs                    Case
Foster      Rawley Martin              Defendant

This came the Plaintiff by his attorney and the Deft in Proper person and the Said acknowledges the Pltffs action therefore it is considered by the court that the Plaintiff recover of the Defendant twenty five Dollars the Debt in the declaration mentioned his costs by him about his Suit in that behalf Stay Ex$^r$ till first Dec.

---

231

            A. L. Duncan               Plaintiff
                vs                     In Case
            Ravley Martin              Defendant

This day came the Plaintiff by his attorney and the Defendant in Proper person and the Said Defendant acknowledges the Plaintiffs action therefore it is considered by the court that the Plaintiff recover against the said Defendant twenty five Dollars the Debt in the Declaration mentioned also his costs by him about his Suit in that behalf expended and the said Defendant in Mercy &c Stay Ex$^{on}$ till first Dec$^r$.

The court nominated and appointed the following persons overseers of the Highways to wit In Captain Morrows District - Thomas Morrow overseer

| Capt$^n$ Barton Hannen | do | Abram _____ | " |
| Capt$^n$ William Darbies | do | William _____ | " |
| Capt$^n$ Benjamine Homes | do | Ebenezer Rees | " |
| Capt$^n$ Israel Luces | do | Caleb King | " |
| Capt$^n$ Joseph Sessions | do | James Howard | " |
| Capt$^n$ Jesse Casten | do | Person Carter | " |
| Capt$^n$ David Greenleaf | do | Sam$^l$ Montgomory | " |
| Capt$^n$ Abram Guice | do | Jonathan Guico | " |
| Capt$^n$ William Nichells | do | Jonathan Dayton | " |
| Capt$^n$ William Voss | do | Anthony Doughorty | " |
| Capt$^n$ Philander Smith | do | Charles Surget | " |

and the clerk is ordered to be certify to each Person of their appointment which the Sheriff is to deliver.

---

232

            Andrew Walker              Plaintiff
                vs
            Jeremiah Bass              Defendant

This day came the Plaintiff by his attorney and the Defendant in Proper Person and mually agree to Dismiss this Suit each Party Paying half the costs accured thereon and Robert by his Atto assumes three Dollars the part of the Plaintiff.

Ordered Court be adjourned till two O'clock.

Court met according to Adjournment
Present
Samuel Brooks
James Neilson
Alexr Montgomery

Ordered that the former Rules at which the Several Tavern Keepers within this County Shall Sell be continued Except that for a Horse at Hay, twenty four Hours they Shall have fifty cents & for one night twenty five cents and the Same is established accordingly.

Robert & George Cochran     Pltffs
    vs
Daniel Lawry     Defendant

By consent of the Parties it is ordered that this Suit be continued till next court.

---

233

Thomas Austin     Plaintiff
   vs
Nathaniel Harrison     Defendant

Reubin Gibson comes into Court and undertakes for the Defendant that in case he be cast in the Suit aforesaid that he shall satisfy and pay the costs condemnations of the court or Surrender his body to Prison in Execution for the Same or in case of failure thereof that he the Said Reubin will do it for him.

         Ferdinand L. Claiborne     Plaintiff
Recorded     vs     In Debt
         Lewis Dunn     Defendant

This day came the Plaintiff by his attorney and the Defendant in Proper Person and the Said Defendant acknowledges the Plaintiffs Action therefore it is Considered by the Court that the Plaintiff recover against the Said Deft fifty eight Dollars and his Costs with interest also his Costs by him about his Suit in this behalf expended & the Sd Defendant in Mercy &c & the Plaintiff agrees to Stay the Execution on this Judgt till the first of November next.

---

234

Ordered by the Court that the Judgt rise against Nathanl Harrison as a Juror be set aside upon his Paying Default The Court nominated and appointed the following persons as Overseers of the Poor in the Several Districts within the County to wit in

| | | | |
|---|---|---|---|
| Captn Robt Morrows | District | Thomas Foster | |
| Captain Barton Hannons | District | William Hoggatt | overseer |
| Captn William Darbies | do | John Grafton | do |
| Captn Benjn Homes | do | Abner Brockham | do |
| Captn Israel Luces | do | David Lambert | do |
| Captn Joseph Sessions | do | James Howard | do |
| Captn Jesse Carters | do | Nathaniel Tomlinson | do |
| Captn David Greenleaf | do | Jeremiah Coleman | do |

(234-236)

| | | | |
|---|---|---|---|
| Capt$^n$ Abram Guice | District | Nathaniel Kinnison | Overseer |
| Capt$^n$ William Nichols | " | Polser Shilling | " |
| Capt$^n$ William Voss | " | Anthony Dougherty | " |
| Capt$^n$ Philander Smith | " | Charles Surget | " |

and the clerk is ordered to certify to each Person of their appointment which the Sheriff to Deliver.

Ferdinand L. Claiborne  Plaintiff
Vs
Alexander Bailey  Defendant

On the Motion of the Defendant Bailey by his attorney at 2 o'clock in the afternoon the first Day of the case to quash the Execution against the said Defendant which is laid over till tomorrow and then to be heard.

Ordered Court be adj$^d$ till tomorrow 9 o'clock.

---

235

Court agreeable to adjournment met
Tuesday 5$^{th}$
Present
Sam$^l$ Brooks
John Henderson
William Darby       Esquires
James Neilson
William Foster
Jacob Guice

Har         Benjamine Kitchens         Defendant
Recorded         vs                    Case
                James Matson           Plaintiff

This day came Benj$^n$ Kitchens the Def$^t$ by his atto and the Plaintiff being Solemnly called comes not nor is his Suit further Prosecuted therefore it is considered by the Court that the Plaintiff be non suited and that the Defendant go hence without day and recover of the Plaintiff his costs by him about his Defence in this behalf

Wal         Thomas Rogan           Plaintiff
Recorded         vs                 case
Har         Benjamine Kitchens     Defendant

W$^d$  This day came the Parties by their attornies and thereupon came a Jury to wit Christian Gilbert Peter Robb, William Glascock, William Clark, John James William Barland Jeremiah Coleman Reubin Newman Samuel Montgomery Abram Taylor Parson Lewis John E. Long.

---

236

Who being elected tried and Sworn well and truly to try the Issue Joined upon their oath do say that the Def$^t$ did asume upon himself in manner and form as the Pltff in his Declaration hath declared and do assess the Pltff Damages by reason thereof to forty eight dollars seventy five cents besides Costs therefore it is considered by the court that the Plaintiff recover against the Said Defendant his Damages aforesaid in Manner and form by the jurers in their verdict aforesaid assessed and his costs by him about his suit in that behalf expended and the Said Defendant in Mercy &c from which Said Judgment the Defendant Prays an appeal to the next Superior Court of Law which is granted him on Payment of costs with his entering into Bond with John Cammack & . Bennett Truly his Sureties in the sum of one hundred and twenty Dollars conditioned as the Law Directs.

  Ferdinand L. Claiborne    Plaintiff
    vs          In Debt
  Benjamine Goodson & A. Bailey Deft

Ordered that the suit be continued till tomorrow by consent.

  William Dunbar Ex$^{tor}$    Plaintiff
    vs
  Andrew Beal      Deft

Continued by consent

---

  Ferdinand L. Claiborne    Plaintiff
    vs          In Debt
  Jacob Nafe       Defendant

Robert Morrow his Special Bail this cause Surrendered up the body of the Defendant in discharge of his recognizance and undertaking & the Said Defendant Prays in Custody & whereupon Avery Clark comes into Court and undertakes for the Defendant that in case he shall be cast in the Suit aforesaid that will pay and Satisfy the costs and conditions of the Court or Surrender his body in Execution to Prison for the Same or in case, of failure thereof that he the Said Avery will do it for him.

  Abija Hunt       Plaintiff
    vs          in Case
  Peter Anthony      Defendant

This day came the parties by their attornies and thereupon came a Jury to wit Christian Gilbert, Peter Robb, William Glasscock, William Clark, John Jures, William Barland, Jeremiah Coleman, Reubin Newman, Samuel Montgomery, Abram Taylor, Parson Lewis, & John E. Long who being elected tried and Sworn well and truly to try the Issue Joined upon

---

Their oath do Say that the Defendant did Promise and undertake in manner and form as the Plaintiff in his Declaration against him hath declared and do assess the Plaintiff Damages by reason thereof to Sixty nine Dollars and Seventy cents besides Costs therefore it is considered by the Court that the Plaintiff recover against the Said Defendant his Damages aforesaid in manner & form by the Jurors in their verdict afore said assessed also his costs by him about his Suit in that behalf expended and the Defendant in Mercy &c

  James Warren      Plaintiff
    vs          In Case
  Thomas Regan      Defendant

This day came the plaintiff by his attorney and Releases the Damages afore said in the Declaration mentioned & prays Judgment for the costs accured on the Said Suit therefore it is considered by the court the Plaintiff have Execution for his Costs afore said according to the form of the Statute in Such case made & preformed.

|                    |           |
|--------------------|-----------|
| A. Hunt            | Plaintiff |
| vs                 |           |
| Jonas Scroggens    | Defendant |
| Same & Smith       |           |
| vs                 |           |
| Same               |           |

Polser Shilling and Charles King come into Court and undertakes for the Defendant that in case he shall be cast in the Suit aforesaid that he shall Satisfy and Pay the costs and condemnations of the court or Surrender his body in Prison for the Same and in case of failure thereof he will do it for him

---

239

Ordered court be adjourned till 2 o'clock.

Court according to adjournment met
Present
Samuel Brooks
John Henderson
James Neilson     Esquires
James Ferrall
W<sup>m</sup> Foster &
Jacob Guice

|                        |                   |
|------------------------|-------------------|
| William McWilliams     | Appellee          |
| vs                     | Appeal from Justice |
| Vansanly Armanda       | Appealant         |
| Bisonto Hernandez      |                   |

By consent of the Parties it is ordered that this Suit be continued.

Wal

|                  |                     |
|------------------|---------------------|
| John Robb        | Appellee            |
| vs               | Appeal from Justice |
| Joseph Gluckland | Appealant           |

This day came the Parties by their attornies and thereupon came a Jury to wit William Gilbert, Peter Robb, William Glascock, William Clarke, John James, William Barland, Jeremiah Coleman, Samuel Montgomery, William Tyler Parson Lewis, John E. Long & Robert Morrow, who being Elected tried and Sworn well and truly to try the Issue Joined upon their oath do say that the appellee hath Sustained Damages by reason of the appealants non performance of the Several Promises and undertakings in the Declaration Specified

---

240

and do assess the Appellee Damages by reason thereof to twenty one Dollars and Seventy five Cents besides costs therefore it is considered by the Court that the Appellee recover against the Appealant his Damages aforesaid in Manner and form by the Jurors in their verdict aforesaid assessed and also his costs by him about his Suit in that behalf expended and the Said appealant in Mercy &c

Garrett Wood & Co.             Plaintiffs
vs
Abram Hill                    Defendant

     William Collins comes into Court and undertakes for the Defendant that in case he shall be cast in the Suit aforesaid that he shall Satisfy and Pay the costs and condemnation of the Court or Surrender his body in Execution to Prison for the Same or in case of failure thereof that the Said William will do it for him.

     Ordered by the Court that all appeals from a Single ~~Justice~~ Magistrates Judg$^t$ to the County Court Shall in future Determined in a Summery Manner at the Same Court at which they are returnable

---

241

Dp     William Mitchell           Plaintiff
            Vs
          Isaac Guilliart   Bail        Deft
Lewis    of Thomas Hutchens

     This day came the parties by their attornies and and the Defendant by his Said attorney acknowledges the plaintiffs action therefore it is considered by the Court that the Pltff recover against the Said Defendant the Sum of one hundred and thirty three Dollars and forty Seven and one half cents Damages including costs.

Har      John Wilkins Jun$^r$         Plaintiff
            vs                           Attachment
Lewis     William Mitchell          Defendant

     Isaac Guilliard Garnishee being Sworn Says that he ows To William Mitchell the Defendant the amt of a Judgment rendered against him at this time as bail of Thomas Hutchins at the Suit of William Mitchell To wit the sum of one hundred and thirty three Dollars and forty Seven and one half cents including costs which sum the said Isaac brings into court and deposits in the hands of the Clerk of the Court Whereupon it is ordered that the Said Isaac be discharged and that the sum of ninety one Dollars & 75 cents remain in the hands of the Said Clerk Subject to the Judgment of the Court.

---

242

Thomas Noble                   Appellee
     vs                           Appeal from Justice Brooks
W$^m$ Darby &               Appealants
John Robb his Surety

     This day came the Plaintiff and the Defendant in Proper Person and the Said Appealant acknowledges the Appellees action for twenty one Dollars and twenty five Cents besides Costs therefore it is considered by the Court that the appellee recover of the appealant and John Robb his Security the sum aforesaid confessed and also his costs by him about his Suit in this behalf and the Said Deft$^s$ in Mercy &c Exon Stayed till Second Saturday in August.

     Ordered by the Court that the County tax be levied on each and every article Taxable and not to exceed that Sum and the Sheriff is hereby ordered to collect Same agreeable to Law.

     Ordered that Court be adjourned till tomorrow morning 9 o'clock.

Wednesday 6th June 1804 Court met agreeable to adjournment Present
James Neilson, Wm Darby, Wm Foster, John Henderson, Alexander Montgomery, Jacob Guice, Esquires

| A. L. Duncan | Plaintiff |
|---|---|
| vs | Attachment |
| Frederick Zerban | Defendant |

The Sheriff having returned that he had levied the Atta{m} herein awarded on
two Set of hand organs in the Possession of Lewis West it is ordered by the
Court by the Said Sheriff Sell them Perishable Property.

In pursuance of the act of assembly in such case made and provided the
Court proceeded to nominate the number of Jurors for the County as directed
by the Said act to attend of the next Superior court whereupon the following
house keepers & free holders were nominated to wit James Foster, Jesse Carter,
Nathan Swayze, John Hutchins John H. White Charles Surget William Booth, A. L.
Benjamine Andrew Walker George Killian William G. Foreman David Holt, Robert
Dunbar Ebenezer Rees David Gibson Ezekiel Newman John Bolls Simon Homes Will-
iam Hoggatt J. W. A. Loyd, Manuiel Maddon Daniel Grafton Thomas Tyler Joseph
Osmun Benj{m} Farrar Jessie Harper George Fitzgerald Thomas Wilkins, Philander
Smith Abram Martin David Greenleaf and John Martin, it is ordered that a
vinere Facias do issue to the Sheriff accordingly.

| Mary Jones | Appellee |
|---|---|
| vs | Appeal from Justice |
| David Berry | Appealant |

The aforesaid appeal this day being called and the Court Proceeded to try
the Same in a Summary manner agreeable to a former rule of this Court upon
consideration whereof the Courts are of the opinion the appellee recover
against the Said appealant fifteen Dollars and fifty cents and the costs
ordered on S{d} appeal

| John Short | Appellee |
|---|---|
| vs | Appeal from Justice |
| Nathan Swayze | Appealant |

The appellee being Solemnly called came not Therefore it is considered by the
court that he be non suited and that the appealant go hence and recover of
the appellee his costs by him about his defence &{c}.

| James Wallace | Appellee |
|---|---|
| vs | Appeal from Justice |
| John Tristler & Williams | Appealants |
| Thompson his Bail | |

This day came the appellee by his attorney and the said appealant failing to
appear and prosecute the Said appeal to effect Whereupon it is considered by
the Court that appellee recover of the appealant & William Thompson his bail
Sixteen Dollars Damages by reason of the Detention of the Same also his Costs
in that behalf expended and the appealant & party in Mercy &{c}

Thomas Austin — Appellee
vs — Appeal from Justice
Wal    Avery Clark & Ann — Appealants
Martin his Bail

This day the aforesaid appeal being called the Said Court Proceeded to try the same in a 2nd Summary way agreeable to a Rule of this Court upon consideration whereof the Court is of the opinion that the appellee recover of the appealant and Ann Martin his Bail the sum of nineteen Dollars Eighty Seven and one half cents the am$^t$ of his note given and also his costs by them about his Suit in that behalf expended.

William Smith — Appellee
vs — Appeal from Justice
Moses Moore — Appealant

This day came the appealant by by his attorney and the appellee being Solemnly called came not therefore it is considered by the Court that the af$^d$ appellee be non Suited and the appealant go hence without day and recover of the appellee his costs by him about his defence in this behalf expended.

Abram Fulkerson — Appellee
vs — Appeal from Justice
John Little & John — Appealant
Callender his Bail

This day the above cause being called the Court Proceeded To try the Same in a Summary way agreeable to a rule of the court & the Judgment thereon & proceedings being examined and inspected by the Court on consideration whereof the Court are of the opinion that the appellee recover of the said appealant and John Callender his bail thirteen Dollars besides his costs by them about his Suit in this behalf expended & the appealant be in Mercy &$^c$

Ordered that Court be adjourned till two o'clock.

Court met according to adjournment
Samuel Brooks
Present
Alexander Montgomery
James Neilson
William Foster
William Darby
Jacob Guice
John Henderson

The court appoints Abner Green David Latimore & William Brooks Inspectors of the Present Election to be held near Benjamine Farrars Mill at the time advertised by the Sheriff of Said County

James Neilson exhibited an account in Court against the Said County which is examined by the Court allowed and ordered to be certified for thirty one Dollars and fifty Cents                $31.50

Ordered that Court be adjourned till tomorrow morning 9 o'clock.

(247-249)

Thursday the 7th 1804 Court agreeable to adjournment met
Present
Samuel Brooks
John Henderson   Esquires
Jacob Guice &
William Darby

Recorded   David Ferguson & Milling Woolley      Pltffs
           vs                                    In Case
           Patrick Connelly                      Defendant

This day came the Parties by their attornies and thereupon came a Jury to wit Christian Gilbert, Peter Robb, William Glascock, William Clark, John James, W<sup>m</sup> Barland, Jeremiah Coleman, Samuel Montgomery, Abram Taylor, Parson Luce, John E. Long, William Morrow, who being elected tried and Sworn well and truly to try the Issue Joined upon their oath do say that the Defendant did assume in Manner and form as the Plaintiff hath declared and do assess the Plaintiff Damages

248

by reason thereof to eight Dollars ninety three and three fourth cents besides costs. Therefore it is considered by the Court that the plaintiff recover against the Said Defendant the Damages aforesaid in Manner and form by the Jurors in their verdict aforesaid assessed and also his costs by him about his Suit in this behalf expended and the Plaintiff by his attorney Prays an appeal to the next Superior Court of Law to be hold for the District of Adams which is granted him with entering into and with Lyman Harding & James Dunlop his Sureties in the Sum of Sixty Dollars conditioned according to Law.

Certified   Jeremiah Coleman, Presented in Court an account ag<sup>st</sup> the County which being Examined by the Court as allowed and ordered to be certified for fifty three Dollars and fifty Cents.   $53.50

Certified   David Gibson the Same for    27.00

           Stephen Stephen Ex<sup>tors</sup>     Plffs
           vs
           Adam Lanehart                 Defendant

Charles King comes into Court and undertakes for the Deft that in case he be cast in this Suit that he will well and truly Pay and Satisfy the Costs and condemnation of the Court or render his body in Prison in Execution for the Same or in case of failure thereof that he will do it for him

249

           Stephen Torry      Plaintiff
           Vs
           John Lusk          Defendant

On the motion of the Plaintiff by his Counsel it is ordered that this Suit be continued at his costs

           John B. Stout      Appealant
           Ads                Appeal
           Ann Martin         Appellee

This day came the Parties by their attornies and the cause being Argued before the Court and the Parties fully heard upon consideration where of the

Court and of opinion that the Judg^t given him by the Justice be confirmed and that appellee recover of the appealant fifteen Dollars and Seventy five cents also his costs by him about her Suit in that behalf expended and the Said appealant be in Mercy &c from which said Judgment the said appealant Prayed an appeal to the next Superior of Law held for the District of Adams which is granted him with giving bond & Security as the Law Directs.

Ordered that court be adjourned till half after two of the clock

Court met half after two according to adjournment

Present
Samuel Brooks
Alexander Montgomery Esq^rs
John Henderson
W^m Darby

| | | |
|---|---|---|
| Wal | William McWilliams | Plaintiff |
| | Vs | In Case |
| Har | Benjamine Kitchens | Defendant |

This day came the Parties by their attornies and thereupon came a Jury to wit Christian Gilbert, Peter Robb, William Glascock, William Clark, John James W^m Barland, Jeremiah Coleman, Sam^l Montgomery, Abram Taylor Parson Lewis, John E. Long & William Morrow who being elected tried and Sworn well and truly to try the Issue Joined upon their oath do say that the Defendant Oweth nothing of the Debt in the Declaration mentioned as in Pleading he hath alledged & find for the Defendant Sixty Seven Dollars and Sixty Six Cents therefore it is considered by the court that the Plaintiff take nothing for his bill but for his false clamour be in Mercy & and that he go hence and recover of the Plaintiff the Sixty seven Dollars and Sixty Six cents in Manner and form By the Jurors in their verdict aforesaid adjudged & also his costs by him about his Defence in that behalf expended.

| | | |
|---|---|---|
| Wal | Anthony Hostman | Appealant |
| | vs | Appeal |
| Lewis | Jacob Nass | Appellee |

Jacob Nass comes here into Court and deposits in the hands of the clerk four Dollars till the final Declaration of the Suit.

| | | |
|---|---|---|
| Lewis | William Murry | Plaintiff |
| | vs | Atto |
| | Thomas Hutchens | Defendant |

This day came the Plaintiff by his attorney and the Plaintiff by his said attorney romits the Damages in his Declaration mentioned except one Cent and Defendant being Solemnly called came not but made Default or doth he say anything in Bar or Purclusion of the Plaintiffs action against him whereby the Pltff remains therein altogeather undefended therefore it is Cons^d by the Court that the Plaintiff recover against the Said Defendant the Sum of nine hundred Dollars the Debt in the Declaration mentioned and one cent Damages and also his costs by him about his suit in that behalf expended and the said Defendant in Mercy &c and it is further ordered that the Sheriff do make Sale of the lands so attached Satisfaction entered this thirteenth Day of October 1804 by order of Pltff^s Atto: Benjamine Seamans Clk.

(251-253)

    Moses Moore                 Appealant
        vs
    Lewis Evans                 Appellee

This day came the Parties by their attornies and cause being Argued before the court and the Parties being fully heard upon consideration whereof the Court are of the opinion that ~~the~~ Judg$^t$ for appealant be confirmed for eighteen Dollars and Seventy five cents & costs of suit from which Judg$^t$ appellee Prayed an appeal which is granted

252

him with giving bonds and security conditioned according to law.

Cert$^d$   Nehemiah Carter makes Oath he attended twelve Days as a witness in Suit Samuel Hutchens against Israel Smith for Defendant & Traveling 72 miles & four ferreages for which he is entitled to fifteen Dollars

    James Ferrall               Plaintiff
        vs
    Joseph B. /Blank/           Defendant

Judgment confessed for am$^t$ of note given with interest & costs and the plaintiff agrees to Stay Ex$^{or}$ till first November

    Thomas Noble             Plaintiff
        vs
    William Darby            Defendant

7$^{th}$ Jan$^{ry}$ 1805 assigned the Judg$^t$ to Thomas Rogan S May

This day came the Plaintiff by his attorney and the Defendant in Proper Person and the Defendant acknowledges the plaintiffs action therefore it is considered by the Court that the Plaintiff recover against the Said Defendant the Sum of one hundred and twenty Dollars also his Costs by him about his Suit in that behalf expended and the Def$^t$ in Mercy &$^c$ & the Plaintiff agrees to Stay Ex$^{en}$ of Judg$^t$ till 2$^{nd}$ Saturday in December

253

On the Motion of John James a Juror Summonsed to attend this Court leave is granted to return home & that he be discharged from Serving on the Jury any more at this term

Ordered Court be adjourned till tomorrow morning nine o'clock.

                          Friday the 8$^{th}$ June 1804
                              Present
                              Samuel Brooks
                              Alexander Montgomery  Esq$^s$
                              and William Darby

    David Ferguson & Milling Woolley     Plaintiff
        vs                                  Case
    Patrick Connally                Defendant

This day came the Parties by their attornies and the S$^d$ Defendant by his attorney waving his former Plea & Saving and reserving to himself every advantage he may have in Equity says he cannot gainsay the Pltffs action against them therefore it is considered by the Court that the Plaintiff recover against the Said Deft the sum of Sixty Dollars with Interest thereon from the first Day of December a Six per Centum Per annum till Paid also his costs by him about their Suit in this behalf expended and the Defendant in Mercy &$^c$ and the Pltff agrees to Stay execution on this Judg$^t$ till next court which damages in that suit make

| | | |
|---|---|---|
| Levi Munsell | | Plaintiff |
| vs | | |
| Robert Mitchell | | Defendant |

Ordered by the Court with the consent of the Parties that a commission Issue in this cause to take the Deposition of Jeremiah Hall Charles Avery and Daniel Sims witnesses in behalf of the Defendant residing out of the Territory on interrogations to be returned and used in Evedence and that Such Commissions be directed to any Justice of the Peace where such witness may reside

| | | |
|---|---|---|
| Abner L. Duncan | | Plaintiff |
| vs | | Atta |
| Frederick Zuban | | Defendant |

Lewis Evans Garnishee being Summonsed answereth Question 1st are you indebted to the Defendant? Answer, I am not, Ques 2nd had you any Property of Said Defendants at the time of serving said attachment - Answer, I had not - Question 3d have you any Property now in your hand of the Said Defendant Answer I have not Ques 4th do you know of any property of Frederick Zubans in the hands of any other Person in the County answer Nothing except two hand organs attached in this Suit. - - -

| | | |
|---|---|---|
| Joseph Martinez | | Pltffs |
| vs | | |
| Hernandes Extors | | Deft |

Ordered a Citation Issue agreeable to the first order made herein

---

| | | | |
|---|---|---|---|
| Wal | Thomas Munfield | | Plaintiff |
| Mahan | Vs | | Atto |
| | David McCleland | | Deft |

This day came the Defendant by his attorney and the Plaintiff being Solemnly called came not therefore it is considered by the court that the Plaintiff be non suited and that the Defendant go hence without day and recover against the Pltff his Costs by him about his suit in this behalf expended

| | | | |
|---|---|---|---|
| Wal | Benjamino Robinson | | Plaintiff |
| Issued | vs | | Trover and Conversion |
| Har | Bennett Truly | | Defendant |

This day came the Parties by their attornies and thereupon came a Jury to wit Christian Gilbert, Peter Robb, William Glascock, William Clark, Moses Moore, William Barland, Jeremiah Coleman, Sam¹ Montgomery, Abram Taylor, Parson Lewis, John E. Long & Robert Morrow who being elected tried and Sworn well and truly to try the Issue Joined upon their oath do say that the Defendant is Guilty of the trover conversion in Manner and form as the Plaintiff hath alledged against him and do assess the Plaintiff damages by reason thereof to one hundred Dollars besides costs therefore it is Considered by the Court that the Plaintiff recover against the Said Defendant his Damages aforesaid in Manner and form by the Jurors in their verdict aforesaid assessed also his costs by him about his Suit in this behalf expended and the Deft in Mercy &c
Recorded

---

Ordered Court be adjourned till 2 of the Clock

(256-258)

                             Court met according to adjournment
                                 Present
                                   Samuel Brooks
                                   Alexander Montgomery   Esquires
                                 & William Darby

Dun     Ex^tors of A. Moore              Plaintiff
            vs                           in Case
Wal     David Phelps                     Defendant

This day came the Defendant by his attorney and the Plaintiff being Solemnly called came not therefore it is considered by the court that the Plaintiff be non Suited and that the Defendant go hence without Day and recover against the Plaintiff his costs by him about his Defence in that behalf expended

Har     Leonard Pomet                    Plaintiff
            vs                           in Case
Def     Bennett Truly                    Defendant
Recorded  This day came the Plaintiff by his attorney and the Defendant in Proper Person and the Defendant acknowledges the Plaintiffs action therefore it is Considered by the Court that the Plaintiff recover against the Defendant the Sum of Seventy three Dollars Seventy Seven and one half Cents and also his costs by him about his suit in that behalf expended & the Deft in Mercy &c

---

                                  257

        Leonard Pomet                    Plaintiff
Recorded    vs                           in Case
        Bennet Truly                     Defendant

This day came the Plaintiff by his attorney and the Defendant in Proper Person and the Said Defendant acknowledges the Plaintiffs action therefore it is considered by the Court that the Pltff recover against the Said Defendant the sum of one hundred and nineteen Dollars also his costs by him about his suit in that behalf expended and the Defendant in Mercy &c it being the am^t of Judg^t S^d Pomet vs Silas L. Payne Dec^d

Pom     George Killian                   Plaintiff
            vs
Recorded, George Lawnig                  Defendant

This day came the Plaintiff by his attorney and Thereupon came a Jury to wit Christian Gilbert, Peter Robb, William Glascock, William Clark, Moses Moore, William Barland, Jeremiah Coleman, Sam^l Montgomery, Abram Taylor, Parson Lewis, John E. Long who being elected tried and sworn well and truly to inquire of Damages in this suit upon their oath do say that the Plaintiff hath sustained Damages by reason of the Defendants non Preformance of his Promise and undertaking in the Declaration mentioned to forty seven Dollars besides costs therefore it is considered by the court that the Plaintiff recover against the Said Defendant his Damages aforesaid in Manner & form by the Jurors in their verdict aforesaid assessed also his costs by him about his suit in that behalf expended & the Deft in Mercy &c

---

                                  258

Har     Stackpool Ex^tors                Pltffs
            vs                           in Case
        William Fletcher                 Defendant
This day came the Plaintiff by his attorney and thereupon came a Jury to wit, (the same Jury) who being elected tried and Sworn well and truly to enquire

of Damages in this Suit Returned Verdict "We of the Jury find for the Plaintiff one hundred and five Dollars and four cents Damages besides Costs" Therefore it is Considered by the Court that the Pltff recover against the Said Defendant his damages assessed in Manner and form by the Jurors in their verdict aforesaid assessed also his costs by him about his suit in that behalf expended and the Said Defendant in Mercy &c

| | | |
|---|---|---|
| Har | David Ewing & Co | Pltffs |
| Recorded | vs | In Case |
| | Bartholomese James | Defendant |

This Day came the Plaintiff by his Attorney and thereupon came a Jury to wit (the same Jury) who being elected tried and Sworn well and truly to Enquire of Damages in this suit Returned verdict "We the Jury find for the Plaintiff fifty four Dollars Damages and Costs of Suit" therefore it is considered by the Court that the Plaintiff recover against the said Defendant his Damages aforesaid in Manner and form by the Jurors in their verdict aforesaid assessed also his costs by him about his Suit in this behalf expended and Deft in Mercy &c

| | | |
|---|---|---|
| Har | William Kenner | Plaintiff |
| Recorded | vs | Att$^a$ |
| | George Lawnig | Defendant |

This day came the Plaintiff by his attorney and thereupon came a Jury to wit, (the same Jury) who being elected tried and sworn well and truly to enquire of Damages in this Suit returned verdict "We of the Jury find for the Plaintiff thirty one Dollars and fifty cents on Damages besides Costs", therefore it is considered by the Court that the Plaintiff recover against the Said Defendant his damages afores$^d$ assessed also his costs by him about his Suit in this behalf expended and the Def$^t$ in Mercy &c

| | | |
|---|---|---|
| Har | James Ferrall | Plaintiff |
| Recorded | vs | In Debt |
| | John M. Huston | Defendant |

This day came the Plaintiff by his attorney and thereupon came a Jury to wit, (the Same Jury) who being elected tried and sworn well and truly to to enquire of Damages in this suit upon their oath do say that the Plaintiff hath sustained Damages by reason of the Defendants non performance of this promise and undertaking in the Declaration Mentioned to fifty nine Dollars besides costs therefore it is considered by the Court that the Plaintiff recover against the said Defendant his Damages aforesaid in Manner & form by the Jurors afs$^d$ assessed also his costs by him about his suit in this behalf Expended and the Deft in Mercy &c

| | | |
|---|---|---|
| Har | Catherine Surget | Plaintiff |
| Recorded | vs | In Case |
| | William Fletcher | Defendant |

This day came the Plaintiff by his attorney and thereupon came a Jury to wit, (the Same Jury) who being elected tried and Sworn well and truly to enquire of Damages in this suit upon their oath do say that the Plaintiff hath Sustained Damages by reason of the Defendants non performance of his

Promise and undertaking in the Declaration mentioned to one hundred & forty
one Dollars and eighty six Cents besides costs therefore it is considered by
the Court that the Pltffs Ex^tors as aforesaid recover of the Defendant the
Damages aforesaid in Manner and form by the Jurors in their Verdict afs^d assessed also his costs the Costs by them about this same suit in that behalf
expended & the Defendant in Mercy &^c

Har  James Ferrall      Plaintiff
Recorded  vs         in Debt
    James Swayze      Defendant

This day came the Plaintiff by his attorneys and thereupon came a jury to
wit (the Same Jury) who being elected tried and Sworn well and truly to enquire of Damages in this Suit upon their oath do say that the Plaintiff hath
Sustained Damages by reason of the non performance of the promise and undertaking in the Decl^n Mentioned & "find for the plaintiff fifty six Dollars
Debt also four Dollars and fifty eight cents Damages which he hath sustained
by reason of the Detention of the Debt besides costs therefore it is considered by the court

---

That the Plaintiff recover against the Said Deft^s the Debt & Damages aforesaid in Manner and form by the Jurors in their Verdict aforesaid assessed
also his costs by him about his Suit in that behalf expended and the Defendant in Mercy &^c

    John Ferrall      Plaintiff
Recorded  vs         In Case
    Elijah Bunch      Defendant

This day came the Plaintiff by his attorney and thereupon came a Jury to
wit (the Same Jury) who being elected tried and Sworn well & truly to enquire of Damages in this Suit upon their oath do say that the Plaintiff hath
sustained Damages by reason of the Defendants non performance of the of his
promises and undertaking in the Declaration Specified to seventy nine Dollars and fifty two cents besides costs therefore it is Considered by the
Court that the Plaintiff recover against the Said Defendant his Damges
aforesaid in Manner and form by the Jurors in their verdict aforesaid assessed also his Costs by him about his Suit in that behalf expended and the said
Defendant in Mercy &^c

---

    Joseph Sheckland    Plaintiff
    vs          In Case
    James Bonnet      Defendant

This day came the Plaintiff by his attorney & thereupon came a Jury to wit
(the Same Jury) who being elected tried and Sworn well and truly to enquire
of Damages in this suit upon their oath do say that the Plaintiff hath Sustained Damages by reason of the Def^t non performance of the Promise and undertaking in the Declaration mentioned to Sixty Dollars besides costs therefore it is considered by the Court that the Plaintiff recover against the
Said Defendant his Damages aforesaid in Manner and form by the Jurors in
their verdict aforesaid assessed also his costs by him about his Suit in
that behalf expended and the Said Defendant in Mercy &^c

| | | |
|---|---|---|
| Wal | Peter Azzavedo | Plaintiff |
| Recorded | vs | In Case |
| Mahan | John Ferguson | Defendant |

This day came the Plaintiff by his attorney and thereupon came also a Jury to wit (the same Jury) who being elected tried and Sworn well and truly to enquire of Damages in this suit upon their oath do say that the Plaintiff hath sustained Damages by reason of the non performance of his Promise and undertaking in the Declaration mentioned to eighty five Dollars and eighty five cents besides Costs therefore it is considered by the Court that the Plaintiff recover against the Said Defendant his damages aforesaid in Manner and form by the Jurors in their verdict aforesaid assessed and also his costs by him about his suit in this behalf and the Deft in Mercy &c

[Endorsed in Margin]
Feby 25th Recd the Amount of the within viz eighty five Dollars and eighty five cents Judgment

Benjamine Stokes,
agent for the Pltff.

[end of Endoresment]

---

263

| | | |
|---|---|---|
| Wal | Francis Killer | Plaintiff |
| Recorded | vs | In Case |
| | Andrew McIntire | Defendant |

This day came the Plaintiff by his attorney and thereupon came a Jury to wit, (the same Jury) who being elected tried and Sworn well and truly to enquire of Damages in this suit upon their oath do say that the Plaintiff hath Sustained Damages by reason of the Defendants non performance of his promise and undertaking in the Decln Specified to forty four Dollars besides costs Therefore it is considered by the Court that the plaintiff recover against the Said Defendant his Damages aforesaid in Manner and form by the Jurors in their verdict aforesaid assessed also his costs by him about his Suit in that behalf expended and the Defendant in Mercy &c

| | | |
|---|---|---|
| Wal | John Short | Plaintiff |
| Recorded | vs | in Case |
| | William B. Smith | Deft |

This day came the Plaintiff by his attorney and thereupon came a Jury to wit, (the Same Jury who being elected tried and sworn will and truly to enquire of Damages in the Suit upon their oath do say that the plaintiff hath Sustained Damages by reason of the Defendants non performance of his promise and undertaking in the Declaration mentioned to one hundred and forty dollars and ninety three and three fourth cents besides costs therefore it is considered by the court that the Plaintiff recover against the Defendant his Damages aforesaid in Manner and form by the Jurors

---

264

Their verdict aforesaid assessed also his costs by him about his Suit in that behalf expended and the Defendant in Mercy &c

| | | |
|---|---|---|
| Wal | John King & Reubin Sackett | Plaintiff |
| Recorded | vs | Covenant |
| | Peter Rucker & Bartholomues | Defendant |

This Day came the Plaintiff by his attorney and thereupon came a Jury to wit, (The Same Jury) who being elected tried and Sworn well and truly to enquire of Damages in this suit upon their oath do say that the Plaintiffs have Sustained Damages by Reason of the Def$^{ts}$ non performance of the Covenants, in the Declaration Specified to Sixty two Dollars besides Costs therefore it is Considered by the Court that the Plaintiff recover against the Said Defendant the Damages aforesaid in Manner and form by the Jurors in their verdict af$^{sd}$ assessed also his costs by him about his suit in that behalf expended and the Def$^{ts}$ in Mercy &c

| | | |
|---|---|---|
| Wal | Ezra Johns | Plaintiff |
| Recorded | vs | Attachment |
| B K | Amos Hubbard | Defendant |

This day came the Plaintiff by his attorney and thereupon came a Jury to wit, (the same Jury) who being elected tried and sworn well and truly to enquire of Damages in this cause upon their oath do say that the Plaintiff hath Sustained Damages therefore "find for the Plaintiff the Sum of three hundred and thirty eight Dollars and twenty five cents the Debt in the Declaration mentioned and one cent in Damages & cost of Suit" Therefore it is considered by the court that the Plaintiff recover against the Said Defendant his Damages aforesaid in Manner and form by the Jurors in their verdict aforesaid assessed also his costs by him about his Suit in that behalf expended & the Defendant in Mercy &c

| | | |
|---|---|---|
| Tur | David Ker | Plaintiff |
| Recorded | vs | In Case |
| | John B Manning | Defendant |

This day came the Plaintiff by his attorney and thereupon came a Jury to wit, (The Same Jury) who being elected tried and Sworn well and truly to enquire of Damages in this suit upon their oath do say that the Pltff hath Sustained Damages by reason of the non performance of his promise and undertaking in the Declaration mention$^d$ to Sixty Dollars besides costs therefore it is considered by the Court that the Plaintiff recover against the Said Defendant his damages aforesaid in Manner and form by the Jurors in their verdict aforesaid assessed also his costs by him about his Suit in that behalf expended and the Def$^t$ in Mercy &c

| | | |
|---|---|---|
| Wal | Reubin T. Sackett & John King | Plaintiff |
| Recorded | vs | In Debt |
| | James Beck & Gibson Johnson | Def$^{ts}$ |

This day came the Plaintiff by his attorney and therefore came also a Jury to wit, (the Same Jury) who being elected tried and Sworn well and truly to enquire of Damages in this Suit Returned the following verdict

"We the Jury find for the Plaintiff Sixty five Dollars the Debt in the Declaration Mentioned and one cent Damages and cost of suit" Therefore it is considered by the court that the Plaintiff recover against the Said Deft$^d$ the Damages aforesaid in manner and form by the Jurors and their verdict aforesaid assessed also his costs by him about his suit in this behalf expended and the Defendant in Mercy &c

| | | |
|---|---|---|
| | Archibald Douglass | Plaintiff |
| Recorded | vs | in Debt |
| | John Lusk | Defendant |

This day came the Plaintiff by his attorney and thereupon came a Jury to wit (the Same Jury) who being elected tried and Sworn well & truly to enquire of Damages in this cause & Returned Verdict for the Pltff for eighty Eight Dollars the Debt in the Decl$^n$ mentioned also eleven Dollars Seventy three and and one third cent Damages which he hath Sustained by reason of the Detention of that Debt also his costs by him about his suit in that behalf expended  Therefore it is considered by the court that the plaintiff recover against the said Defendant his damages aforesaid in Manner and form by the Jurors in their verdict aforesaid assessed also his costs by him about his Suit in that behalf expended and the Deft in Mercy &c

266

|  | | |
|---|---|---|
| | John Robb | Plaintiff |
| Recorded | vs | In Debt |
| | Exsor Capshaw | Defendant |

This day came the Plaintiff by his attorney & thereupon came a Jury to wit (the Same Jury) who being elected tried and Sworn well and truly to enquire of Damages in this suit returned the following Verdict "We the Jury find for the Plaintiff the Sum of one hundred and fifteen Dollars the Debt in the Declaration mentioned and one cent Damages & costs of Suit" therefore it is considered by court that the Plaintiff recover against the Said Defendant his Damages aforesaid in Manner and form by the Jurors in their verdict aforesaid in Manner and form by the Jurors in their verdict aforesaid assessed also his costs by him about his suit in that behalf expended and the said Defendant in Mercy &c

Ordered by the Court that the following Strays be Sold under the Direction of Alexander Montgomery to wit one Brown Cow & Calf, a red heifer and two year old Steer reserving one third of the net Proceeds of the Sale to William Chaney the Latter up for his services in herding them Several years also two Stray heifers taken up by Jeremiah Coleman reserving also one third Part of the net Proceeds to the S$^d$ Jeremiah for his trouble in herding the Said cattle.

| Joseph Strickland | Plaintiff |
|---|---|
| vs | In Debt |
| James Bennet | Defendant |

On the motion of the Plaintiffs attorney it is ordered by the Court that the writ of enquirey & verdict of Jury be set

| Moses Moore | Appealant |
|---|---|
| vs | |
| Lewis Evans | Appellee |

Ordered that the Judgment of this suit be Dismissed and the appellee Hereto discharged.

A return of the commissioners appointed to lay off the Prison Bounds was this day made and approved by the court and ordered to be recorded.

Ordered by the Court that the Sheriff of this County Complete the Collection of the County tax for this County for the year 1805 that is to say on all objects of Taxation to one half the am$^t$ of the territorial Tax on which Such objects are Subject and Pay the Same into the County treasury agreeable to law and that this order be entered as at the last term in December hence Pro time having then been omitted by Clerical mistake

James Wallace Esq$^r$ Produced an Acc$^t$ against the County of Adams for Surveying the Prison Bounds and returning a map of the Same amounting to twenty five Dollars which being examined is allowed & ordered to be certified for                             $25.00

Ordered by the Court that the List of Taxable Property be corrected in the list returned by William Darby Esq^r to wit the Taxation one Billiard table and that the money which appears to have been collected

267

by the Sheriff be returned by the Said Sheriff John McGuire the Said tax not having been legally

W^m Nicholls having given Bond with approved Securities to this Court conditioned for the Collection of the Tax for this Current Year agreeable to Law which Said Bond are ordered to be transmitted to the Treasurers Authorized to receive the Same

David Ferguson & Melling Wooley Plaintiff
    vs
Anthony Calvet                 Defendant

This day came the Plaintiff by his attorney and the Defendant by his atto and the Defendant acknowledges the Plaintiffs action for Therefore it is considered by the court that the Plaintiff recover against the Said Defendant the Sum of and also his costs by him about his Suit &c

John Holly
    vs                    The death of the defendant sug-
James Campbell            gested the papers in file Dec
Term 1804 Supa against Adm^r Samuel Postlewaite & returned (Scirefeci)

/Page 268 missing/

269

aside and an alias ordered returnable next court

Ordered that a committee of three Persons be appointed and find the most eligible Situation for Building a Perminent Bridge over the St Catherine Creek at or about ~~at or about~~ the Present Crossing Place on the road leading from Natchez to Washington and Determine on the Kind of Bridge to be built and reserve Proposal for Building the Same and report thereof to the next county Court, John Henderson, James Neilson & William Brooks Esquire appointed accordingly.

Ordered that Court be adjourned till tomorrow morning eight O'clock.
                          Saturday 9th 1804, Court met according
                          to adj^mnt
                               Present
                               Samuel Brooks
                               John Henderson
                               William Darby     Esq^rs
                               & Neilson

Benj^m Robinson            Plaintiff
    vs                       In Trover
Bennett Truly               Deft

The Defendant by his attorney and motioned the court the Verdict & Judg^t made herein by Def^t aside and a new trial
/MS torn: a line missing/

Name and Subject Index

(Abr-Bin)

Abrams, Andrew, 113, 115, 117, 118, 119, 120, 121, 122, 123
Abrams, Robert, 18
Accounts, County, 66, 67, 69, 110, 112, 131, 133, 134, 136, 139, 154, 171, 184, 185, 188, 197, 215, 227, 247, 248, 266
Acres & McBride, 190, 209
Adair, Stephen, 200
Adams, Andrew, 116
Adams County, dividing line between Jefferson and Wilkinson Counties and, 110
Adams, District of, jurors nominated to the superior court of the, 23, 154
Adams, Elisha, 168
Adams, John, 61
Admission of attorneys, 1, 74, 82, 98, 110, 128, 192, 227
Alexander, Isaac, 80
Allison, David, 154
Alston, Phillip, Junr, 178
Andrews, Arthur, 127
Andrews, James, 2, 70, 71, 72
Anthony, Peter, 152, 163, 200, 237
Antoni, Figaro, 171
Appointments
  of road
    overseers, 8, 80, 231
      viewers, 7, 12, 24, 28, 35, 44, 75, 114, 217
  of overseers of the poor, 57, 234
Apprentices, 45, 57, 227
Armanda, Vansanly, 239
Armstreet, John, 7, 146, 149, 150, 153, 156, 159, 163, 170
Ashland, Sam¹, 143
Ashlock, Benjamine, 144
Ashlock, Samuel, 83
Ashworth, James, 47
Atchinson, William, 117
Atchison, 108
Attorneys, admission of, 1, 74, 82, 98, 110, 128, 192, 227
Augustin, Francisway, 155
Austin, Thomas, 233, 245
Avory, Charles, 254
Azzavedo, Peter, 262

Bailey, Alexander, 234, 236
Baker, Love, 70, 71, 91, 130, 147, 161, 202
Balk, Benjn, 329
Banks, Sutton, 15, 23, 29, 68
Barbour, David, 106
Barland, 108
Barland, William, 20, 42, 154, 235, 237, 239, 247, 250, 255, 257,
Barney, David, see Burney
Barney, John, see Burney
Barr, Henry, 123
Barr, James, 29, 63
Barrow, William, 50, 76, 77, 124
Bartholomues, 264
Barton, Margaret, 178
Bashford, Robert, see Baskford
Baskford (Bashford), Robert, 134, 143, 171, 174, 179
Bass, James, 24
Bass, Jeremiah, 1, 5, 203, 232
Beal, Andrew, see Beall
Beal, Rich<sup>d</sup>, 199, 200
Beall (Beal), Andrew, 150, 190, 199, 200, 236
Beardman, Charles, 229
Beauvais (Beauverais, Beauvias, Beauvies), St. James, 61, 92, 95, 106, 125, 140, 151, 159, 161, 168, 172, 208
Beauverais, St. James, see Beauvais
Beauvias, James, see Beauvais
Beauvies, St. James, see Beauvais
Beck, James, 264
Beckham (Brockham, Buckham), Abner, 154, 155, 187
Bell, Andrew, 24
Bell, Jesse, 146, 149, 150, 153, 156, 159, 163, 173, 174, 179
Bell, Joseph, 175
Bell, William, 20
Benedict, Anthony, 31
Benjamine, Adam, see Bingamin
Benner, Willis, 178
Bennet, James, 262, 266
Bergamin, Adam, see Bingamin
Berry, David, 244
Berry, Thomas, 219
Bingamin (Benjamine, Bergamin), Adam, 68, 187, 229, 243

(Bla-Cam)                      Name and Subject Index

Blanchard, John, 222
Blumon (Blumor), James, 18, 45, 58
Blumor, James, see Blumon
Boles, Claiborn, 164
Boles, John, see Bolls
Bolls (Boles, Bowles, Bowls), John, 24, 80, 99, 137, 146, 149, 150, 153, 156, 159, 163, 170, 173, 174, 179, 243
Bonel, Elias, see Bonnell
Bonel, Mary 35
Bonnell, 79
Bonnell (Bonel), E. (Elias), 8, 34, 35
Bosley, James, 92
Bosley, John, 105
Boundary lines between Adams, Jefferson, and Wilkinson Counties, 110
Bowger, Henry, 224
Bowles, John, see Bolls
Bowls, John, see Bolls
Boyd, Samuel, 88, 93, 219, 221, 225, 226
Brabston, John, 44
Bradish, Ebenezer, 107
Bradish, E. M., 98
Bradley, John, 7, 154
Bradshaw, John, 228
Bragg, William, 210
Brandon, Jerry, 216
Brands, marks and, 83, 130, 132, 135
Brenburg, William, 227
Bridges, 228, 269
Brocher, William, 92
Brockham, Abner, see Beckham
Brookes (Brooks), William (Will), 72, 75, 126, 151, 154, 155, 156, 168, 182, 216, 246, 269
Brooks, Anthony, 72
Brooks, Justice, 242
Brooks, Samuel (Sam¹), 1, 7, 15, 22, 27, 37, 38, 40, 46, 59, 73, 82, 88, 93, 98, 107, 111, 128, 131, 134, 136, 137, 138, 144, 151, 154, 157, 162, 164, 166, 170, 171, 174, 183, 185, 186, 191, 193, 197, 201, 202, 204, 212, 221, 225, 228, 232, 235, 239, 246, 247, 249, 253, 256, 269

Brooks, William (Will), see Brookes
Brow, John, 30
Brown, William, 71
Bruin, Peter Bryan (Brian), 29, 32, 163, 164, 166, 179, 185
Bruin, William, 102
Bryan, Ferd, 121
Bryan, John, 228
Buckham, Abner, see Beckham
Bullen (Bullin), John, 15, 53, 68, 77
Bullin, John, see Bullen
Bunch, Elijah, 251
Burling, Walter, 48, 187
Burnet, Lewis, 86
Burnett, John, 98
Burney (Barney), David, 75, 80, 112
Burney, James, 13
Burney (Barney), John, 170, 173, 182
Buskirk, 57
Buskirk, Jane, 57
Bustrick, John, 113

Calhoun, John, 82
Callendar, John, see Callender
Callender (Callendar), John, 57, 73, 88, 93, 107, 111, 130, 134, 186, 191, 201, 202, 225, 246
Calligam, John, see Callihan
Callihan (Callihan, Calligam), John, 78, 88, 89, 93, 95, 97, 100, 106, 108, 113, 115, 116, 117, 118, 119, 120, 121, 122, 123
Callihan, John, see Calliham
Calvet, Alexander, 12
Calvet, Anthony, see Calvit
Calvet, Frederick, 12
Calvet, John, see Calvit
Calvit (Calvet), Anthony, 95, 97, 98, 146, 220, 267
Calvit (Calvet), John, 146
Calvit, Joseph, 34
Calvit, Montford, 3, 10, 11, 16, 18, 50, 60
Calvit, Phebe, 30
Cammack (Cammick), John, 30, 113, 115, 116, 117, 118, 119, 120, 121, 122, 123, 137, 172, 236
Cammick, John, see Cammack

Name and Subject Index (Cam-Con)

Campbell, James, 267
Campbell, John, 173, 174, 176, 179
Campbell, Patrick, 165
Campbell, T., 165
Capshaw, Esox (Exser), 165, 266
Carmicheal, John F., 87
Carmick, George, 95
Carney, Arthur, 121
Carpenter, James, 61, 229
Carradine, Parker, Sen$^r$, 142
Carrick, James, 22
Carrol, Benjamin (Benjamine), 2, 29, 75
Carroll, Moses, 64, 148
Carter, Captain, 78, 132
Carter, J$^o$sse, 8, 12, 79, 80, 234, 243
Carter, Nemiah (Nehemiah), 79, 252
Carter, Parson, 192, 197, 214, 215, 220, 221, 222, 223, 224, 231
Carter, Robert, 36
Carton, Seth, see Caston
Cast, James Lewis, 207
Caston, Capt. Jesse, 231
Caston (Carton), Seth, 69, 128, 142, 218
Caston, Charles, 148
Cavalier and Petit, 2
Cayson, Charles, 208, 209, 210, 211
Chaney, Barley, 28
Chancy, Batley E., 7
Chaney, William, 266
Childers (Childress), Robert, 80, 154
Childress, Robert, see Childers
Churchill, Henry, 201
Churchwell, 90
Claiborne (Claiborn), Leonard (Leo), 43, 75, 91, 183
Claiborne (Claiborn), Capt. Ferdinand L., 21, 35, 40, 41, 48, 59, 67, 111, 128, 137, 138, 151, 154, 171, 195, 216, 219, 228, 233, 234, 236, 237
Claiborne (Claiborn), William C. C., 74, 82, 98, 110, 128, 138, 182
Claiborn, Ferdinand L., see Claiborne

Claiborn, Leonard, see Claiborne
Clairborn, William, see Claiborne
Clark, Connally &, 174, 184
Clark, Avery, 237, 245
Clark, William, see Clarke
Clarke, Daniel, 97, 103
Clarke (Clark), William, 76, 82, 88, 89, 93, 95, 97, 100, 106, 108, 113, 115, 116, 117, 118, 119, 120, 121, 122, 123, 129, 235, 237, 239, 247, 250, 255, 257
Cobb, Arthur, 81, 139, 188, 192
Cochran, 134
Cochran (Cockran), Robert, 93, 166, 185, 232
Cochran (Cockran), William, 82, 90, 100, 106, 108, 113, 115, 116, 117, 118, 119, 120, 121, 122, 123, 129, 187, 231
Cochran, George, 3, 4, 38, 107, 116, 232
Cochran, John, 62
Cochran, Nathaniel, 108
Cochran, Phebe, 90
Cochran, Thomas, 90
Cockefair, Elijah, 212
Cockran, Robert, see Cochran
Cockran, William, see Cochran
Cole, James, 7, 193
Coleman, James, 70
Coleman, Jeremiah, 8, 234, 235, 237, 239, 247, 248, 250, 255, 257, 266
Collins, William, 240
Compton, John, 226
Compton, Leonard B., 195
Compton, Philip R., 226
Congill, John, see Cowgill
Connally, Clark &, 174, 184
Connally, Patrick, see Connelly
Connelly (Connally, Connoly), Patrick, 6, 39, 51, 63, 68, 73, 91, 92, 94, 99, 101, 102, 108, 114, 151, 156, 159, 170, 173, 174, 175, 183, 196, 198, 203, 229, 247, 253
Connely, Patrick, see Connelly
Conner, Arthur, 2
Conner, John, 156
Conner, William, 12

(Cor-Eld)  Name and Subject Index

Corey (Kories, Koris), Job, 4, 139, 188
Cory (Kories, Koris), Richard, 4, 139, 188
County
  accounts, 66, 67, 69, 110, 112, 131, 133, 134, 136, 139, 154, 171, 184, 185, 197, 215, 227, 247, 248, 266
  dividing lines between Jefferson and Wilkinson Counties, 110
  tax levy, 242, 266
Courthouse, court considers it has no right to levy a tax to build, 202
Cowgill (Congill), John, 192, 197, 214, 215, 220, 221, 222, 223, 224
Crabb, Thomas, 203
Craig, 131
Craig, Elijah, 24, 72
Craig, James, 141
Croker, John, 197
Cromer, Frederick, 147
Crow (Crowe), John, 10, 11, 140
Crowe, John, see Crow
Custard, Morris, 10, 63, 193, 194

Darbies, William, see Darby
Darby (Darbies), William, 22, 23, 111, 128, 130, 131, 132, 138, 157, 166, 169, 174, 193, 197, 201, 202, 219, 225, 226, 227, 231, 234, 235, 242, 246, 247, 249, 252, 253, 256, 266, 269
Darby, George, 210
Darcy, Benjamine, 154
Daugherty, Anthony, see Dougherty
David, John, 88
Davis, Hugh, 74
Davis, Jonathan, 85, 153, 157, 176
Dayton, Jonathan, 154, 231
Declarmount, Joseph, 154
Deeds recorded, 2, 3, 4, 9, 15, 19, 36, 38, 39, 40, 44, 48, 50, 61, 67, 69
Derrock (Dorrock), Thomas, 55, 118
Dewit, Ezekiel, see Dewitt

Dewitt (Dowit), Ezekiel, 3, 10, 16, 17, 18, 19, 21, 22, 24, 27, 30, 31, 32, 36, 37, 41, 43, 49, 50, 59, 76, 82, 84, 88, 89, 93, 95, 97, 100, 106, 108, 113, 129, 154, 227
Dewitt, John, 56
Dick, James, 59
Dinwiddy, James, see Dunwoody
Donalson & wife, 83
Dorrock, Thomas, see Derrock
Dougherty (Daugherty), Anthony, 44, 69, 110, 154, 195, 231, 234
Douglass, 129
Douglass, Archibald, 265
Douglass, Daniel, 65, 71, 84, 92, 142, 146, 194, 196
Douglass, Stephen, 13, 44, 149, 150, 183
Dowling, Charles, 160, 196
Downs, Richard, 74, 222
Duhamil, John, 167
Dunbar, James, 187
Dunbar, Robert, 23, 24, 80, 243
Dunbar, William, 15, 79, 125, 199
Dunbar, William, Jr., 1, 5, 181, 187, 190, 203, 236
Duncan, Abner L. (A. L.), 3, 9, 40, 60, 131, 155, 230, 231, 243, 254
Duncan, Capt., 24
Duncan, H. L., 77
Dunlap (Dunlop), James, 41, 94, 180, 248
Dunlop, James, see Dunlap
Dunn, Lewis, 233
Dunwoody (Dinwiddy), James, 44, 59, 72
Duvell, James, see Duvill
Duvill (Duvell), Lewis, 144, 211

Earhart, Jacob, 154
Eastis, Elijah, see Estis
Elam, William B., 17
Eldergile, John, see Eldergill
Eldergill (Eldergile), John, 30, 31, 39, 41, 43, 84
Eldridge, Elisha, 43

Name and Subject Index (Ele-Gea)

Election, inspectors of appointed, 246
Elliott, James, 52
Ellis, Hardress, 29, 75, 86, 124
Ervin, Thomas, see Irwin
Erwin, Joseph, see Irwin
Erwin, Thomas, see Irwin
Estis (Eastis, Estridge), Elisha (Elijah), 3, 10, 11, 16, 18, 22, 25, 27, 30, 31, 32, 33, 36, 37, 41, 154, 187
Estrays
  Appraisement of, 155,
  sale of ordered, 266
Estridge, Elisha, see Estis
Evans, 125, 210
Evans, Archabald, 146, 149, 150, 153, 156, 159, 163, 170, 226
Evans, Lewis, 20, 35, 68, 69, 70, 128, 138, 142, 152, 158, 163, 198, 202, 251, 254, 266
Evans and Overaker, 70
Ewing, David, 258

Farrar, 78, 132
Farrar (Farrow), Alexander, 7, 69, 107, 146, 204
Farrar (Farrow), Benjamine, 7, 243, 246
Farrall, James, see Ferrall
Farrell, James, see Ferrall
Farrell, John, see Ferrall
Farrill, James, see Ferrall
Farrow, Alexander, see Farrar
Farrow, Benjamine, see Farrar
Forgett, Charles, 136.
Ferguson, David (Davis), 9, 86, 90, 91, 103, 115, 117, 140, 150, 154, 157, 167, 189, 198, 247, 253, 267
Ferguson, John, 18, 33, 50, 121, 181, 262
Ferguson, Mrs., 9
Ferguson & Wolley (Woqley), 13, 86, 90, 91, 103, 115, 117, 177, 200, 217
Ferrall (Farrall, Farrell, Farrill), James, 1, 7, 74, 92, 93, 100, 111, 136, 138, 139, 191, 193, 201, 202, 220, 223, 230, 239, 252, 259, 260
Ferrall (Farrell), John, 91, 261
Ficundas (Fiocundus), Jacob, 75, 97
Fielding, Denny, 164

Findlay, James, see Findley
Findley (Findlay), James, 13, 75, 90, 91
Fiocundus, Jacob, see Ficundas
Fisher, Elias (Elisha), 6, 89, 104, 189, 194
Fitzgerald, 130
Fitzgerald, George, 35, 190, 243
Fitzgerald, John, 149
Flannigan, James, 177
Fletcher, William, 109, 258, 260
Flower, 100
Flower (Flowers), Samuel, 43, 48, 49, 62, 93
Flowers, Samuel, see Flower
Foley, Patrick, 22, 36, 78, 87, 102
Ford & Reed, 55, 142, 227
Ford, John, 28
Ford, Joseph, Sr., 48, 49, 80
Ford, Thomas, 76, 82, 88, 89, 93, 95, 97, 100, 106, 108, 113, 115, 116, 117, 118, 119, 120, 121, 122, 123, 129, 192, 197, 214, 215, 220, 221, 222, 223, 224
Foreman, William, see Forman
Forman (Foreman), William G., 23, 243
Foster, James, 24, 187, 243
Foster, John, 44, 76, 88, 89, 93, 95, 97, 100, 106, 108, 113, 115, 116, 117, 118, 119, 120, 121, 122, 123, 129, 171
Foster, Thomas, 187, 231, 234
Foster, William, 23, 24, 80, 136, 174, 183, 186, 216, 219, 221, 225, 226, 228, 235, 239, 242, 246
Fowler, Daniel, 217
Freeman, Thomas, 60
Fulkerson, Abram, 246

Galbraith, William N., 27
Galtney (Gartney, Gaultney), Abraham, (Abram), 76, 82, 88, 89, 93, 95, 97, 129
Garrach, John, see Garrett
Garrett (Garrach), John, 24, 138
Gartney, Abraham, see Galtney
Gaultney, Abram, see Galtney
Gearaighty, Philip, 40

(Gib - Hon)                                         Name and Subject Index

Gibson, David, 24, 60, 80, 112, 133, 140, 154, 157, 220, 221, 222, 223, 224, 243, 248
Gibson, Reubin (Reuben, Rubin), 11, 22, 24, 25, 27, 30, 31, 32, 33, 36, 37, 42, 43, 50, 60, 192, 197, 214, 215, 220, 221, 222, 223, 224, 233
Gilbert, Christian, 235, 237, 247, 250, 255, 257
Gilbert, William, 4, 139, 188, 239
Gilliard (Guilliart), Isaac, 79, 154, 241
Gillick, Reubin, 125
Girault, John, 114
Glascock, William, 235, 237, 239, 247, 250, 255, 257
Glass, Robert, 105
Gluckland, Joseph, 239
Goodson, Benjamine, see Goodwin
Goodwin (Goodson), Benjamine, 143, 236
Grafton, Daniel, 135, 243
Grafton, John, 23, 187, 234
Grafton, Thomas, 154
Grass, Anthony, 178
Grayton, Capt. Richard, 59
Green, 129
Green, Abner, 12, 40, 44, 48, 98, 107, 111, 128, 132, 134, 142, 246
Green, Charles B., 227
Green, Henry, 142, 194
Green, James, 30, 65, 71
Green, Thomas, 142
Greenfield, Jesse, 49, 75, 80
Greenleaf, Captain, 217
Greenleaf (Greenlief), David, 7, 82, 88, 89, 93, 95, 97, 217, 229, 231, 234, 243
Greenlief, David, see Greenleaf
Griffin, Absalom, 137, 154
Griffin, James, 171
Griffin, Joseph, 148, 214
Grinnell, Thomas, 110
Guice, Abram, 28, 192, 197, 214, 215, 220, 221, 222, 223, 224, 231, 234
Guice, Capt., 8, 28, 80
Guice, Christopher, 28
Guice (Guise), Jacob, 7, 15, 22, 27, 111, 201, 213, 235, 239, 242, 246, 247

Guice, Jonathan, 138, 144, 151, 154, 157, 162, 164, 216, 231
Guilliart, Issac, see Gilliard
Guion, Isaac, 127, 187
Guise, Jacob, see Guice

Hadley, Joshua, 227
Hall, Jeremiah, 254
Hames, Joshua, 72
Hamilton, Cyrus, 84
Hamilton, George, 150
Hamilton, Jesse, 84
Hancock, Regan, Timberlake &, 97
Hancock, Samuel Timberlake &, 104, 126
Hancock, Sam¹., 76
Hancock, Timberlake &, 30, 63
Hanes, Thomas, 112
Hannon, Barton, 124, 221, 231, 234
Harding, Lyman, 2, 3, 15, 57, 74, 135, 248
Harmon, Barton, 155, 166
Harmon, Christian, 112, 149, 163, 170
Harmon, Christopher, 146, 150, 153, 156, 159, 173, 174, 179
Harmon, Joseph, 157
Harper, Jesse, 7, 28, 243
Harris, Edwin L. (Edmund), 90, 147
Harris, Joseph, 5
Harrison, Joseph, 140, 228
Harrison, Nathaniel, 193, 233, 234
Harris, Thomas, 173, 182
Harvard, David, see Havard
Havard (Harvard), David, 140, 157, 168, 181, 192, 197, 214, 215, 220, 221, 222, 223, 224
Hawley, Daniel, 197
Headey, Samuel, 19
Headies, Ezekiel, see Heady
Heady (Headies), Ezekiel, 112, 134
Henderlider, Martin, see Hinderlider
Henderson, Walker &, 208
Henderson, Alexander, 67
Henderson, John, 1, 15, 19, 27, 46, 59, 66, 69, 73, 82, 85, 91, 92, 128, 131, 132, 134, 137, 138, 144, 160, 164, 166, 171, 174, 183, 184, 186, 191, 201, 203, 204, 212, 213, 216, 228, 235, 239, 242, 246, 247, 249, 269
Honery, William, 223

Name and Subject Index (Hon-Jam)

Henry, John, 224
Hernandes, 254
Hernandez, Bisente, 239
Hieth, Thomas, 221, 222, 223, 224
Higdon, Jeptha, 217, 218, 219
Highway overseers, appointment, 8, 80, 231
  See also Road; Roads
Hill, Abram, 240
Hinderlider (Henderlider), Martin, 85, 88, 143, 197
Hindman, Samuel, 167
Hinds, John, 76
Hogg, David Johnson &, 213
Hogg, James, 50
Hogg, James, & I. B. Theri, 181
Hoggart, Anthony, see Hoggatt
Hoggart, Wilford, see Hoggatt
Hoggatt, 221
Hoggatt (Hoggart), Anthony, 24, 80, 154
Hoggatt, Jas., 85
Hoggatt, John, 195
Hoggatt, Nathan, 187
Hoggatt, Phillip, 149, 150, 159
Hoggatt (Hoggart), Wilford, 24, 155
Hoggatt, William, 187, 234, 243
Hoggett, McClure &, 9
Hogland, Isaac, 11
Holland, 126
Holland, John, 6, 37, 38, 74, 151, 182, 189
Holley (Holly), John, 67, 134, 176, 267
Holly, John, see Holley
Holmes (Homes), Benjamine, 80, 155, 231, 234
Holmes, Simpson, 24
Holston, Henry, 118
Holt, David, 24, 187, 243
Homes, Benjamine, see Holmes
Homes, Simon, 243
Hook, Benjamine, 144
Hook, Simon, 144
Hopkins, Gideon (Goderen), 7, 139, 146, 149, 150, 153, 156, 159, 163, 170
Hopper, Jesse, 7
Horton, Richard, 86
Hostman, Anthony, 250

House, Thomas, 168
Howard, David, 76, 82
Howard, Given, 112
Howard, James, 79, 231, 234
Howard, Joseph, 80
Howard, Joshua, Jun$^r$, 187, 237
Hubbard, Amos, 162, 264
Huffman, Martain, 52
Hunt, Abijah (Abjah, Abija, A.), 57, 84, 94, 99, 101, 102, 104, 114, 120, 153, 159, 163, 181, 200, 222, 237, 238
Hunt, A. & Smith, 238
Huston, John M., 259
Hutchens, Thomas, see Hutchins
Hutchins, Anthony (A.), 40, 130
Hutchins, Col., 78
Hutchins, John,
Hutchins, Samuel, 132, 252
Hutchins (Hutchens), Thomas, 28, 39, 46, 65, 88, 101, 241, 251
Hutsell, William, 76, 82, 88, 89, 93, 95, 97, 100, 106, 108

Inspectors of election appointed, 246
Irvin, Joseph, see Irwin
Irwin, John, 76, 80, 82, 88, 89, 93, 95, 97, 100, 106, 108, 111, 113, 115, 116, 117, 118, 119, 120, 121, 122, 123, 129, 138, 154, 155, 175
Irwin (Ervin, Irvin), Joseph, 1, 7, 73, 154, 155, 157, 162
Irwin (Ervin, Erwin), Thomas, 55, 148, 169, 183, 208, 209, 210, 211
Ivy, Nathaniel, 19

Jail
  See also Prison bounds
  court considers it has no right to levy a tax to build, 202
  inspection of ordered, 68
  repairs to, 68, 110
James, Bartholomese (Barth$^m$), 10, 258
James, Henry 84
James, John, 235, 237, 239, 247, 250, 253

(Jef-Lin)                                    Name and Subject Index

Jefferson County, dividing line between Adams County and, 110
John, Ezra, 152, 162, 168, 264
Johnson & Hogg, David, 213
    See also Johnston
Johnson, Gibson, 264
Johnston (Johnson), David, 72, 133, 146, 161, 213
Johnston, Thomas, 152
Johnston, William, 169
Jones, Francis, 15, 41
Jones, James, 49
Jones, John, E., 189
Jones, Mary, 244
Jurors nominated to the superior court for the district of Adams, 23, 154
Justices, appointment of to receive lists of taxable property, 111

Keller (Killer), Francis, 85, 196, 263
Kelly, James, 227
Kemper, Smith &, 183
Kemper, Reuben, 158
Kennady, David, see Kennedy
Kennedy (Kennady), David, 77, 176, 203
Kenner, William, 50, 104, 147, 160, 184, 194, 259
Ker, David, 17, 41, 139, 190, 264
Kerr, Lewis, 1
Kiddy, Moses, 170, 173, 174, 179
Killer, Francis, see Keller
Killian, David, 187
Killian, George, 3, 10, 11, 16, 18, 22, 25, 41, 43, 50, 60, 153, 156, 159, 162, 168, 170, 173, 174, 179, 243, 257
Killian, Joseph, 153, 156, 159, 162, 163
Kimson, William, 28
Kin, Charles, see King
King, Caleb, 7, 15, 80, 98, 111, 231
King (Kin), Charles (Ch$^s$), 83, 89, 137, 139, 146, 211, 238, 248
King, George, 40, 41
King, John, 3, 10, 11, 16, 18, 22, 25, 27, 30, 31, 32, 36, 37, 41, 43, 48, 50, 59, 77, 115, 129, 143, 264

King, Maj. Richard, 35, 100, 179, 187
King, Prosper, 8, 99
King and Sacket, 83
Kinnison, Nathaniel, 7, 28, 234
Kirkland, Richard, 6
Kirkpatrick, Patrick, 152
Kitchens (Kitchez), Benjamine, 29, 57, 71, 85, 91, 92, 114, 120, 121, 122, 123, 127, 128, 130, 146, 149, 153, 163, 164, 166, 176, 183, 198, 199, 235, 250
Kitchens & Smith, Benj$^n$, 85
Kitchez, Benjamine, see Kitchens
Knilton, Jno., 123
Knox, Robert, 25
Kories, Job, see Cory
Kories, Richard, see Cory
Koris, Job, see Cory
Koris, Richard, see Cory

Labrathra, John Baptist, 120
Lambert, David, 234
Lanehart, Adam, 248
Langford, John W., 214
Laslie, Panton & Co., 185
Latimore (Lattemore), David, 110, 227, 246
Lattemore, David, see Latimore
Lauck, Isaac, 110
Lawin, George, see Lawnig
Lawing, George, see Lawnig
Lawnig (Lawin, Lawing), George, 40, 133, 162, 168, 184, 208, 257, 259
Lawry, Daniel, 232
Lee, Christopher, 30, 31, 61, 63, 99, 167, 171, 193, 196
Lee, Joseph, 74, 79, 222
Leland, William, 230
Lemon, William, 23, 216
Lennox, James, 31
Leonard, Israel, 192, 197, 214, 215, 220, 221, 222, 223, 224
Lewis, Abrabel, 2
Lewis, Archibald, 24, 61, 217
Lewis, Parson, 235, 237, 239, 250, 255, 257
Lewis, Seth, 74, 132
Lewis, William, 61
Lintot (Lintott), William, 76, 82, 88, 89, 93, 95, 97, 100

Name and Subject Index (Lin-Min)

Lintott, William, see Lintot
Little, John, 246
Loaman, William, 110
Loan, William, 108, 114
Loftes, Panton, & Co., 179
Lomak, James, 17
Long, John E., 10, 11, 140, 141, 179, 189, 198, 214, 216, 235, 237, 239, 247, 250, 255, 257
Loopez, Manuel, see Lopez
Lopez (Loopez), Manuel, 99, 196
Lougham, Michael, 105
Loyd, Elijah, 172
Loyd, Joseph, W. A., 204, 243
Luce (Luse), Capt. Israel, 3, 7, 10, 11, 16, 18, 22, 25, 27, 30, 31, 32, 36, 37, 50, 59, 120, 231, 234
Luce, Parson, 247
Luse, Capt., 7
Luse, Capt. Israel, see Luce
Lusk, John, 7, 204, 249, 265
Lusk, Samuel, 1, 154

McBride, Acred &, 190, 209
McBride, Andrew, 195
McBride, Charles, 66, 129, 133, 224
McCabe, Rebecca (Rebekah), 28, 39, 43, 48, 65, 68, 90, 95, 101
McCammack, William, see McCormick
McCann, Nicl, 129
McCibbin, James, 21
McCleland, David, 178, 255
McCleland, Walter, 170, 174, 179
McClure & Hoggatt, 9
McCollum, Hansel (Hamel, Hansol, Hornself), 3, 10, 16, 18, 22, 25, 27, 32, 33, 36, 37
McCormick (McCammack), William T., 29, 41, 69, 90, 127
McCoy, John, 154
McCullock, Martin, 169
McCullock, Mathew, 116
McDowell, Samuel, 41
McDuffy, Archibald, 77
McGrath, James, 71
McGuire, John, 267
McGurley, John, 10
McIntire, Andrew, 263
McIntosh, Eunice, 178

McIntosh, James, 23, 154, 187
McIntosh, William, 154
McMullen, Daniel, 95
McMullen, James, 2, 19
McNoelley, 133
McNeely, James, 113
McWilliams, 57, 127
McWilliams, Martin, 73, 110
McWilliams, William (W$^m$), 63, 146, 177, 199, 239, 250

Madden, Emanuel (Manuiel), 23, 243
Mahan, Samuel S., 4, 31, 35, 38, 173
Maloney, Edward, 86
Malson, James, 176, 180
Manning, John B., 264
Marks and Brands, 83, 130, 132, 135
Marschalk (Marshalk), Andrew, 4, 24, 136
Marshalk, Andrew, see Marschalk
Martin, Abram, 3, 60, 102, 231, 243
Martin, Ann, 17, 21, 82, 84, 165, 181, 214, 245, 249
Martin, John, 7, 76, 80, 82, 88, 89, 93, 95, 97, 100, 106, 108, 113, 115, 116, 117, 118, 119, 120, 121, 122, 123, 129, 217, 229, 243
Martin, Nancy, 200
Martin, Pheba (Phebe, Phoebe), 4, 93, 109
Martin, Rowley, 230, 231
Martin, Thomas (Toman), 11, 35
Martinez, Joseph, 176, 203, 254
Massey, Thomas, 52
Mathews, James A., 133
Matson, James, 111, 235
May, Richard, 88
May, Samuel, 137, 155, 252
Melson, James, 21
Monsantos (Monsantos), Benjamine, 5, 70, 140
Michie, David, 38, 66
Milian, Francisco, 54
Miller, Christopher, 24
Miller, Richard, 129
Minyard, Barnaba, 226

(Mit-Par)  Name and Subject Index

Mitchell, David, 12, 79, 222
Mitchell, John, 82, 87, 192, 197,
    215, 220, 221, 223, 224
Mitchell, Robert, 254
Mitchell, William, 6, 46, 241
Moffett, Darius, 43, 59
Monola, Babptest, 207
Monsantoes, see Monsantos
Monsantos, Benjamine, see Monsantos
Montgomery, Alexander (A.), 11, 204,
    216, 219, 221, 224, 228, 232,
    242, 246, 253, 256, 266
Montgomery, Samuel, 217, 231, 235,
    237, 239, 247, 250, 255, 257
Montgomery, William, 192, 193, 197,
    214, 215, 217, 249
Moore, 83, 90, 134, 169, 178, 179
Moore, Alexander (A.), 29, 118, 256
Moore, James, 17, 78, 129, 187
Moore, Lewis, 173
Moore, Michael, 86, 181
Moore, Moses, 3, 10, 11, 16, 18,
    22, 25, 27, 30, 31, 32, 33, 36,
    37, 41, 43, 50, 59, 72, 115,
    116, 117, 118, 119, 120, 121,
    122, 123, 149, 150, 153, 156,
    159, 163, 170, 175, 201, 245,
    251, 255, 257, 266
Moore, Robert, 28, 38, 40, 65, 86,
    154, 160, 187, 209
Moore, Samuel P., 78, 113, 129
Moore, Thomas, 82
Moore, W., 178
Morris, John, 102
Morris, Samuel, 15, 44
Morrow, Capt. Robert, 217, 234,
    237, 239, 255
Morrow, William, 247, 250
Mulhallon, William, 103
Muncey, William, 92
Munfield, Thomas, 178, 255
Munsell, Levi, 254
Murray, William, 88, 251

Nafe, Jacob, 237
Nailor, Frances, 211
Nass, Jacob, 250
Neil, Samuel, 24
Neillson, James, see Neilson
Neilson (Neillson, Nielson), James,
    27, 44, 48, 59, 67, 71, 73, 82,

Neilson (Neillson, Nielson), James,
    (cont.), 111, 115, 128, 131, 138,
    144, 154, 157, 174, 177, 228, 232,
    235, 239, 242, 246, 247, 269
Neilson, Samuel, 126
Newman, Benjamine, 217, 229
Newman, Ezekiel, 243
Newman, Joseph, 24, 72, 83
Newman, Reubin, 235, 237
Nicholls, Thomas, see Nichols
Nicholls, William (Wm.), 131, 171,
    184, 185, 188, 231, 234, 267
Nichols, John, 40
Nichols (Nicholls), Thomas, 19, 56
Nicklass, John, 50
Nielson, James, see Neilson
Noble, Thomas, 242, 253
Nolin, William, 9
Noname, Philip, 114
Norwood, Charles, 229
Null, Samuel, 146, 174

O'Conner, John, 107, 109, 116
Odair, Stephen, 165
Ohara, Timothy, 63
Oliver, Mary, 67
Ormsby, Joseph B., 149
Orrilly, Richard, 40
Orr, James, 1, 5
Osburn, Benijah, see Osmun
Osman, Benijah, see Osmun
Osmun (Osburn, Osman), Benijah,
    75, 243
Ousteen, Moses, 221
Overaker, Evans and, 70
Overaker, George, 35
Overaker, John, 43, 75, 173, 220
Overseers
    of highways, 8, 80, 231
    of the poor, 57, 234
Owens, Martin, 19, 49
Owens, Samuel, 12

Pain, Benjamin, 157
Pain, Silas L., see Payne
Palmer, Archabald, 92
Panett, Leonard, see Ponet
Pannell, Joseph, 154
Panton, Laslie & Co.; 185
Panton, Loftes & Co., 179
Parker, John, 196

Name and Subject Index (Par-Rob)

Parkison, Robert, 187
Park, Robert, 180
Parks, Culberson, 180
Patterson, Robert, 174, 179
Payne (Pain), Silas L., 218, 257
Payne, Winneford, 178
Pearson, Henry, 41
Pendergraft, Garrett E., see Pendergrast
Pendergrass, Garrett, see Pendergrast
Pendergrast (Pendergrass, Pendergraft), Garrett E., 85, 100, 141, 143
Perkins, 134
Perkins, John P., 20, 116, 120, 136, 173, 174
Perkins, Joseph, 15, 36
Perkins, J. P., 184
Perrelliatte, James, 54
Perrelliatte, John, 54
Perry, Roderick, 216
Perry, Robert, 216
Petit, Cavalier and, 2
Phelps, David, 256
Phillips, David, 142
Phipps, 107
Phipps, Henry, 119
Phipps, Samuel, 2
Pillory, whipping post, and stocks, 136
Pipes, Windsor (Winsor), 53, 68
Plain, Edward, 141
Poindexter, George, 128
Pomet, 133
Pomet (Pamett), Leonard, 59, 113, 257
Poor, overseers of, 8, 57, 80, 234
Pope, Wm., 226
Porter, Alexander, 50
Postlethwait (Postlewaite), Samuel, 29, 267
Postlewaite, Samuel, see Postlethwait
Potter, John, 32
Presley, Peter, 12
Price & Whiting, 164
Price, William, 77
Prison bounds, 73, 112, 133, 212, 266
  See also Jail

Rabb, Nicholas, 192, 197, 214, 215, 220, 221, 222, 223, 224
Rabb, Peter, see Robb
Ragan, Thomas, see Regan
Ranor, Daniel, 61
Ranor, Mrs., 61
Rapalie, George, see Rapalje
Rapalje (Rapalie), George, 4, 141, 172, 179, 189, 198
Rapllee (Replee), John, 114, 210
Rasselly, John, 51
Rates, tavern, 81, 232
Recorded deeds, 2, 3, 4, 9, 15, 19, 36, 38, 39, 40, 44, 48, 50, 61, 67, 69
Reed, Ford &, 55, 142, 227
Reed, John, 136
Reed, Martha, 99
Reed, Thomas, 159
Reeds, Mrs., 140
Rees, 132
Rees (Reese), Ebenezer, 16, 19, 20, 21, 24, 31, 41, 42, 44, 59, 69, 70, 81, 113, 115, 139, 144, 148, 149, 158, 188, 192, 204, 211, 214, 231, 243
Reese, 98, 125
Reese, Ebenezer, see Rees
Regan, Timberlake, & Hancock, 97
Regan (Ragan), Thomas, 83, 106, 122, 128, 147, 176, 199, 235, 238, 252
Reid, Thomas, 24
Replee, John, see Rapllee
Reynolds, Samuel, 6, 74
Richey, 96
Road
  overseers, appointment of, 8, 80, 213
  viewers
    appointment of, 7, 12, 24, 28, 35, 44, 75, 114, 217
    reports of, 8, 78, 79, 85, 111, 112, 130, 132, 229, 230
Roads, 7, 8, 12, 23, 24, 28, 35, 44, 75, 78, 79, 80, 85, 111, 112, 114, 130, 132, 217, 229, 230, 231
Robb, John, 239, 242, 266
Robb (Rabb), Peter, 193, 235, 237, 239, 247, 250, 255, 257

(Rob-Stu)  Name and Subject Index

Robinson, Andrew, 122
Robinson, Benjamine, 185, 225, 255, 269
Rodrigrees, Juan, 36
Roe, William, 71
Routh (Ruth), Jeremiah, 8, 22, 25, 27, 30, 31, 32, 33, 36, 37, 41, 43, 44, 114, 221
Routh, Job, 24, 35
Rucker, Jonathan, 7
Rucker, Peter, 264
Ruth, Jeremiah, see Routh
Ryan, Daniel, 77

Sacket, King and, 83
Sackett, Reubin (R), 143, 264
Sargent, Winthrop (Wynthrop), 18, 45, 58, 106, 134
Saxon, Moses, 87
Sayze, Nathan, see Swayze
Scott, John, 91, 97
Scott, William, 2, 243
Scroggens, Jonas, 238
Seamans, Benjamine (B), 90, 155, 188, 227, 229, 251
Searcy, Asa (Asey), 162, 166
Sessions, Joseph, 44, 88, 110, 111, 136, 137, 231, 234
Sessions, Richard, 187
Shackelford, Rowland, 172, 220
Shackler, John, 50, 170
Shockland, Joseph, 262
Shelton, Lewis, 34, 35, 177
Sheras, George, 173
Sherley, David, 64
Shields, William B., 192
Shilling, Polser, 43, 234, 238
Short, John, 244, 263
Shunk, Elizabeth, 5
Shuto, John, 219
Sible, John, 79
Sigvalt, Tomasinan (Thomasina), 11, 35
Silkreg, William, 96
Sims, Daniel, 254
Singleton, Joseph, 150, 210
Smith, A. Hunt &, 238
Smith, Benj. Kitchens &, 85
Smith & Kemper, 183
Smith, Calvin, 187

Smith, Hughey, 52
Smith, Israel, 12, 86, 142, 154, 252
Smith, John, 134
Smith, Philander, 12, 72, 75, 142, 231, 234, 243
Smith, William B. (WM.), 27, 28, 84, 125, 161, 162, 202, 227, 245, 263
Smith, Wm. B. Jun$^r$., 214, 215
Snow, Ebenezer, 89
Sojourner, Lewis, 87
Sollivellas, (Sollivillas), Miguel, 24, 61, 72, 193
Sollivillas, Miguel, see Sollivellas
Spring, Simon, 89
Stackpoole, 107, 258
Stackpool, Maurice, see Stackpoole
Stackpoole (Stackpool), Morris (Maurice), 29, 107, 118, 119, 140, 161, 165, 190, 202
Stagel, Jacob, 168
Stanfield, Robert, 133
Steele, Col. John, 28, 35
Stevenson, Ezekiel, 33
Stevenson (Stephenson), Steven (Stephen), 27, 30, 31, 32, 36, 95, 100, 106, 108, 162, 199, 211, 248
Stephenson, Stephen, see Stevenson
Stewart, 115
Stewart, James, 12
Stillee, John, 33
Stocks, pillory, and whipping post, 136
Stokes, Whiting &, 50
Stokes, Benjamine M., 6, 106, 134, 262
Stout, John B., 249
Stricker, Barent, 67
Strickland, 114
Strickland, Joseph, see Strickland
Strickland (Strikland), Joseph, 86, 145, 173, 174, 179, 266
Strikland, 134
Strong, Joseph, 76, 82, 88, 89, 143, 144
Strother, Arthur, 87
Stubbefield, Washington, see Stubblefield
Stubberfield, Washington, see Stubblefield

Name and Subject Index (Stu-Vie)

Stubblefield (Stubbefield, Stubberfield), Washington, 113, 115, 117, 118, 119, 120, 121, 122, 123
Sulcer, George, 110
Sullivan, Thomas, 148
Superior Court for the District of Adams, jurors nominated to, 23, 154
Surget, Catherine, 260
Surget, Charles, 112, 168, 187, 231, 234, 243
Surveyor, appointment of, 110
Swayze, Gabriel (Gab), 120, 154, 187
Swayze, James, 260
Swayze, John, 139
Swayze, Nathan Junr., 163
Swayze, Richard, 7
Swayze (Sayze), Nathan, 7, 80 110, 146, 150, 153, 156, 159, 163, 170, 243, 244
Swayze, Solomon, 212
Sweaney, John, 171

Tally, John, 169, 209
Tarsadu, Manuel, 84
Tavern
  licenses
    recommended, 59
    granted, 73, 85, 99, 137, 193, 216
  rates, 81, 232
Tax
  court considers it has no right to levy, to build courthouse and jail, 202
  levy, county, 242, 266
Taxable property, justices appointed to receive lists of, 111
Taxes, collection of, 242, 266
Tayler, William, 239
Taylor, Abram, 3, 10, 11, 16, 18, 27, 30, 31, 32, 33, 36, 37, 42, 43, 50, 60, 62, 192, 197, 235, 237, 247, 250, 255, 257
Taylor, John T., 187
Terry, Stephen, 204, 249
Thamburgh, Bartholemus, 100

Theri, I. B., James Hogg &, 181
Thery, Hogg &, 180
Thomas, Julian, 189
Thompson, 96
Thompson, William, 148, 172, 183, 220, 244
Throgmorton, Robert, 3, 10, 11, 12, 13, 16, 18, 22, 24, 27, 30, 31, 32, 33, 36, 37, 41, 43, 50, 60.
Thyre, Benjamine, 189
Tilcot, Ezekiel, 183
Timberlake & Hancock, 30, 63
Timberlake & Hancock, Regan, 97
Timberlake, Samuel, 30, 62, 63, 79, 103, 104, 124, 154, 173, 174, 179, 211
Timberlake, Samuel, & Hancock, 104, 124
Tomlinson, 78, 98
Tomlinson, Nathaniel, 24, 25, 43, 48, 68, 70, 93, 129, 142, 154, 218, 234
Tolley (Tooly), Adam (A), 83, 112, 193, 197, 201, 204, 213, 219
Tooly, Adam, see Tooley
Trask, Israel, 75
Tristler, John, 244
Truly, 115
Truly, Bennet (Bennett, Bennotte), 13, 44, 62, 100, 106, 149, 150, 153, 154, 156, 173, 174, 179, 184, 185, 225, 236, 255, 257, 269
Turner, Henry, 5, 68, 90, 96, 110, 131, 161
Tyler, Thomas, 2, 44, 47, 98, 243

Valcourt, Lewis, 190, 209
Vamet, Ezekiel, 157
Vandorn, Peter A., 91, 115, 116, 117, 118, 119, 218
Vandorn, William A., 12
Vansant, Ezekiel, 153
Verdiman, John, 7
Vidal, Juan, 126
Viewers, road
  appointment of, 7, 12, 24, 28, 35, 44, 75, 114, 217
  reports of, 8, 78, 79, 85, 111, 130, 132, 229, 230

(Vos-Zub)  Name and Subject Index

Voss, Capt. William, 231, 234,
Vousdan, William, 41, 165, 190

Wade, Capt. John, 24
Walker & Henderson, 208
Walker, Andrew, 3, 10, 11, 16, 18,
  22, 25, 27, 30, 31, 32, 36, 37,
  41, 43, 75, 187, 232, 243
Walker, Peter, 23, 35, 108, 116
Walker, Peter, Jun$^r$., 137, 138
Wallace, James, 11, 39, 62, 98, 113,
  140, 181, 198, 244, 266
Walton, John, 207
Ward, Frederick, 84
Ward, Thomas, 8
Ware, James, 65
Warren, James, 175, 238
Watson, Samuel, 9, 187
Weisger, 114
Weisiger, Daniel, 145
Wells, 126
Wells, John, 4, 10, 27, 37, 93,
  100, 131, 156, 168, 182
Wells, William, 9, 29
West, James, 146, 149, 150, 153,
  155, 159, 163, 170, 192, 197,
  214, 215, 220, 221, 222, 223,
  224
West, Lewis, 24, 243
West, Little Berry, 208
Wheatley, Richard, 74
Whipping post, stocks, and pillory,
  103
Whitaker, Daniel, 3, 10, 11, 16, 18,
  22, 24, 25, 27, 30, 31, 32, 33,
  36, 37, 41, 43, 50, 60, 154, 217,
  229
White, Andrew, 2
White, Hampton, 12, 79
White, John H. (Jn$^o$ H.), 80, 243
White, Mathew, 4
Whiting, Price &, 164
Whiting & Stokes, 50

Whiting, Luke (Lake), 13, 124,
  126, 160
Whitton, John, 176
Wiley, James, 152, 163, 202
Wilkins, Beman B., 11
Wilkins, Charles, 59, 94
Wilkins, James, 38, 147, 158
Wilkins, John Jun$^r$, 241
Wilkins, Thomas, 16, 23, 124, 187,
  199, 243
Wilkinson County, dividing line
  between Adams County and, 110
Wilie, John, see Wylie
Williams, 8
Williams, George, 83
Williams, William, 154
Williamson, James, 29
Willis, Aseneth (Asseneth), 69, 79
Willson, 100
Willson, John, see Wilson
Willson, Robert, see Wilson
Wilson, James, 198
Wilson (Willson), John, S, 60, 91,
  97, 140, 142, 198
Wilson (Willson), Robert, 171, 207
Winery, Lewis, 73
Withers, Jesse, 203
Wood, Garrett, 240
Wooley (Woolley), Ferguson &, 13,
  86, 90, 91, 103, 115, 117,
  177, 200, 217
Wooley (Woolley), Melling, (Milling),
  3, 107, 150, 198, 247, 253, 267
Woolley, Milling, see Wooley
Wooley, see Wooley
Wylie (Wilie), John, 23, 61, 62

Yirzer, Jacob, 97
Young, 108

Zerban (Zuban), Frederick, 9, 243,
  254
Zuban, Frederick, see Zerban

www.ingramcontent.com/pod-product-compliance
Lightning Source LLC
Chambersburg PA
CBHW020654300426
44112CB00007B/382